LUTHERAN
VOICES

Give Us This Day
A Lutheran Proposal for Ending World Hunger

Craig L. Nessan

Augsburg Fortress
Minneapolis

GIVE US THIS DAY
A Lutheran Proposal for Ending World Hunger

Direct Scripture quotations are from New Revised Standard Version Bible, copyright © 1989 Division of Christian Education of the National Council of the Churches of Christ in the United States of America. Used by permission.

Editors: Scott Tunseth and Rochelle Melander

Cover Design: Koechel Peterson and Associates, Inc., Minneapolis, MN
        www.koechelpeterson.com

Cover photo: Koechel Peterson and Associates, Inc.

ISBN 0-8066-4993-3

The paper used in this publication meets the minimum requirements of American National Standard for Information Sciences—Permanence of Paper for Printed Library Materials, ANSI Z329.48-1984.

Manufactured in the U.S.A.

07   06   05   04   03   1   2   3   4   5   6   7   8   9   10

Contents

The Prayer of the Children

By Kurt Bestor

Can you hear the prayer of the children,
On bended knee in the shadow of an unknown room?
Empty eyes with no more tears to cry,
Turning heavenward toward the light.

Crying Jesus, help me to see the morning light—of one more day!
But if I should die before I wake, I pray my soul to take.

Can you feel the hearts of the children,
Aching for home—for something of their very own?
Reaching hands with nothing to hold onto,
But hope for a better day—a better day.

Crying Jesus, help me to feel the love again—in my own land.
But, if unknown roads lead away from home, give me loving arms—
away from harm.

Can you hear the voice of the children,
Softly pleading for silence in a shattered world?
Angry guns preach a gospel full of hate –
Blood of the innocent, on their hands.

Crying Jesus, help me to feel the sun again—upon my face.
For when darkness clears, I know you are near, bringing peace again.

Can you hear the prayer of the children?

Foreword

Give Us This Day is a timely book for people of faith, and for Lutherans in particular. For the first time in history, we have the ability to end widespread hunger in God's world. Craig Nessan aims his impassioned call that we do just that at Christians in an affluent society that tempts us (as he admits he is tempted) to "a theology that makes [us] comfortable in a world where the poor are invisible."

Drawing on his own experience, the author puts a face on hungry and poor people in our cities and towns and in developing countries. More than that, he weaves a vivid thread of biblical imperatives to present the elimination of hunger as a theological imperative of the highest priority for Christians in response to God's grace. Readers will especially appreciate his exegesis of the Lord's Prayer as an unambiguous call to neighbor love and our sharing of bread. His most direct challenges to action are grounded both in a knowledge of policy issues that confront us in our resolve to end hunger, and in the specific ways in which Lutheran theology and church history call us to act.

This book will find a receptive audience, as has Bread for the World, among Lutheran church leaders and members. Lutherans in America have demonstrated a strong commitment over many years to overcoming world hunger. The main Lutheran church bodies have all maintained vigorous hunger programs for thirty years. These are popular programs; Lutherans have been consistently generous not only in their giving but in leading advocacy efforts to reduce hunger. This is partly because so many Lutherans live in farm states, so they especially feel the scandal of persistent hunger in contrast to food production. While Bread for the World is very broadly interdenominational, it is not entirely coincidental that both persons who have served as president of Bread for the World are Lutheran pastors.

Craig Nessan's message that concern for food and hungry people is at the heart of Christian mission, and the bold voice in which he raises unsettling issues of wealth, food distribution and conscience, place him in a long line of practical prophets. Bread for the World welcomes his voice. This readable book will be passed around in wide circles of people who are seeking to be faithful in a challenging global community.

DAVID BECKMANN, PRESIDENT
Bread for the World

Preface

"For you always have the poor with you, and you can show kindness to them whenever you wish." (Mark 14:7) Do you think Jesus might look back and regret this saying, considering how it has been misinterpreted over the centuries? This one verse has been used all too often as an excuse for justifying the continuing plight of the poor and hungry in our world. Careful interpretation would show that Jesus did not intend this saying to serve as a rationalization for our sloth in relationship to the needs of the poor but rather as a call to action on their behalf!

We live in a world where nearly one billion hungry neighbors struggle daily to survive. This book examines what the Bible has to say about God's concern for the poor and hungry (Chapter One), giving special attention to the prayer Jesus taught to his disciples, the Lord's Prayer (Chapter Two). We will hearken to the testimony of those who live and minister among the hungry in other parts of the global Christian community (Chapter Three). In light of God's Word and the acute needs of the hungry, this book argues that at this moment in history the church should declare ending hunger a core element of Christian faith, a matter of *status confessionis* (Chapter Four). Ending hunger in our time is a real possibility, requiring an intensification of efforts on the part of the church in both development projects and advocacy (Chapter Five). Jesus Christ sets us free by the power of the Gospel to act on behalf of the hungry (Conclusion). The book ends with a sermon postscript, a short bibliography. Each chapter concludes with study questions for reflection and discussion.

We live in a time of increasing alarm over national security and fear of terrorism. In my study over the years I have devoted serious attention to the reasons for discontent in other parts of the world, leading to the emergence of movements for liberation. While the "wretched of the earth" (Fanon) themselves are seldom the primary actors in perpetrating terrorism or organizing revolutionary movements, it is the cause of the poor that fuels those ideologues who do turn to acts of violence in an attempt to provoke political and economic change. *In no way do I myself condone any act of violence.* If, however, we are to begin to comprehend the dynamics that lead to terrorism, we need to pay attention to the disparity in our world between rich and poor that gives rise to anti-Western ideology. In terms consistent with the argument of this book, we need to address in a constructive way the needs of the hungry, if we are to live in a more secure world for all.

There are many people I desire to thank for their assistance in this project. Kevin Anderson, Mary McDermott, LaDonna Ekern, and Tiffany Nichole Broman have provided valuable help at Wartburg Theological Seminary in various stages of preparing the manuscript and discussion questions. I want to thank my colleague, Professor Shannon Jung, Director of the Center for Theology and Land, for timely consultation and for sharing with me the draft of his own book, *Food for Life: Eating and the Goodness of God*, to be published by Fortress Press in 2004. At Augsburg Fortress, Scott Tunseth has been a wonderful editor and Michael West has provided long-term support for this project. I am grateful to Ralph Klein, editor of *Currents in Theology and Mission*, and to Carl E. Linder and William A. Decker, editors of *Lutheran Partners*, in which journals portions of this book were published in an earlier form as essays. The impetus for this book was generated by an invitation to speak at a gathering of the Conference of Bishops of the Evangelical Lutheran Church in America about the proposal that ending hunger become a matter of *status confessionis*, a situation in which faithfulness to God's

Word requires giving confessional status to an issue normally considered secondary to the gospel. I continue to be thankful for the encouragement I received from them for completing this manuscript.

All royalties from the sale of this book are being donated to Bread for the World and the ELCA World Hunger Program.

I dedicate this book to the children of the world, including my own children—Ben, Nate, Sarah, Andrew, Jessica, and Mary Catherine—praying that God will empower the church to feed their hunger.

Craig L. Nessan
Pentecost 2003

Introduction
Discovering the World of the Hungry

When I was a small boy growing up in Lansing, Michigan, we had to drive down Logan Street (now named after Martin Luther King) to get to the grocery store that my Uncle John managed. This is a street on which Malcolm Little, later named Malcolm X, lived for a short time as a boy. As I looked out the window of the car, I saw dilapidated houses and poor black children playing next to the busy street. It's the first time I remember asking myself the question, "Why?"

When I was a teenager, I recall watching pictures of people living in abject poverty. Pictures flashed across the screen as I listened to reports on television covering the voter registration drives in southern towns. Even more disturbing, I remember being in Detroit for a Tigers game the day the riots started there and that evening seeing pictures of the world of the poor, this time burning down. Again I asked myself: "Why?"

There have been many periods of time, some of them rather lengthy, when I stopped asking the question, "Why?" Other concerns and priorities pressed to center stage—personal and professional. Had my life taken a different course, I can easily imagine that the images of poverty that troubled me in my youth would have become submerged deep beneath my daily existence. I very much understand how it is possible to live life, engaged in concerns that keep one detached from the world of the hungry. Every day I am tempted to construct such a life in which the poor become absent. I am also tempted to construct a theology that makes me comfortable in a world where the poor are invisible.

As an adult, however, I have had the opportunity of visiting places like Mexico, Nicaragua, and India, and the images and encounters from these visits will not leave me alone. On the Mexico trip, I enjoyed the privilege of the company of Bishop Charles Maahs (Central States Synod, ELCA) and his son, David. In Cuernavaca we met Angela in a squatters village of 4000 called *La Estacion*, literally on the other side of the tracks. Angela cared there for an invalid husband, receiving a little income from seasonal farm labor, selling Coca-Cola, crafting needlework in a co-op, and from grown children in California who sent her money. What sticks with me the most about our visit with Angela was a comment about her roof. The rainy season was coming and she was worried because she was going to have to give her roof back to its owner from whom she had borrowed it. Can you imagine living with a borrowed roof? Outside children played along filthy sewage ditches and in houses constructed, in many places, of discarded asbestos siding.

Then there was Manuel in a Mexican village. He introduced his family by saying he had ten children. Then he explained that three of them had died as infants. He said this matter-of-factly, as though it was perfectly normal to have three of your ten children die from the diseases of the poor.

Lawrence is a pastor and theology teacher in Madurai, South India. One afternoon he took me on a walking tour visiting his neighborhood. I saw family after large family living in narrow quarters—6, 8, 10, 12 persons to a room. Everywhere I saw thin, malnourished children and emaciated elderly people. Many lived at the edge of the streets. In Nicaragua we drove by the shacks of those who lived on the garbage dump of the capital city of Managua, scraping a living from the refuse.

These are experiences that will not leave me alone. No matter how I try to leave them behind—Angela, Manuel, the people of Madurai, and the staring faces in Managua—these hungry neighbors accompany me wherever I go. Enrique Dussel writes:

The . . . painful scream resulting from a blow, wound, or an accident indicates immediately not *something* but rather *somebody*. One who hears the cry of pain is astonished because the scream interrupts the commonplace and integrated world. The sound, the noise, produces a mental image of an absent-present somebody in pain. The hearer does not know as yet *what kind* of pain it is, nor the reason for the outcry. But the hearer will be disturbed until he knows who is crying out and why. *What* that cry says is secondary; the fundamental issue is the cry itself; one who is *somebody* is saying something. It is not what is said but rather the saying itself, the person who cries out, who is important.[1]

I begin my reflections, if you will, with a scream—a scream on behalf of the hungry children of Lansing, Cuernavaca, and Tamilnadu. I still cannot fully answer the question "why" they are hungry, although I have my theories. But I can use my privileged voice to scream in pointing to them. Initially, that's what proposing stopping hunger as a matter of *status confessionis* means to me: a way of screaming on behalf of the hungry. We are baptized members and leaders of the Christian church in the richest and most politically influential country of the world. The biblical tradition in which we stand establishes defense of the poor, widow, orphan, and stranger as a fundamental obligation. Together we must find the voice to respond to their scream.

Questions for reflection and discussion

1. The quote by Enrique Dussel distinguishes between "some body" and "some thing." How and when do bodies (i.e., people) become things (i.e., objects)?
2. What prevents your hearing the cries of the hungry?

1

Biblical Witness: The Justice Tradition

How can we pray for daily bread, with lip
Still smacking from a comfortable meal,
Or how, from Dives lofty table feel
With Lazarus the glow of fellowship,
Unless, with spirits destitute, we find
Fellowship in the deserts of the mind.

THERE IS A SPIRIT: THE NAYLER SONNETS by Kenneth Boulding,
© Pendle Hill Publications. Used by permission.

All Bible verses are not created equal. As Lutherans, we should know well this hermeneutical assertion. The Lutheran Reformation and tradition was founded on the proposal that within Scripture the truth of justification by grace through faith alone is that crucial article upon which all else depends. We are justified by faith in God's gracious saving act in the life, death, and resurrection of Jesus Christ. Our sins no longer are counted against us but rather, for Jesus' sake, Christ's righteousness is reckoned to us. The Holy Spirit works faith in us to enable us to trust in Christ's saving work. The gospel for Reformation Sunday declares:

". . . If you continue in my word, you are truly my disciples; and you will know the truth, and the truth will make you free" (John 8:31-32).

Set free for love of neighbor

To be justified by grace through faith is to be set free. Paul's voice echoes from his letter to the Galatians, "For freedom

Christ has set us free" (5:1). And Martin Luther in his treatise on "The Freedom of a Christian" insisted: "A Christian is a perfectly free lord of all, subject to none."[1] Among twentieth century scholars, perhaps no one has better captured the essence of this evangelical insight than Ernst Käsemann with the title of his New Testament study: *Jesus Means Freedom.*[2]

The radical freedom of the gospel of Jesus Christ is a dangerous thing. It shatters every attempt to demonstrate our worthiness from any other source. We must beware of all attempts to temper its radicality. The freedom of the gospel means that because my sins are forgiven for Christ's sake, I need not exist paralyzed by guilt. The freedom of the gospel means I need perform no pious rituals to secure salvation, since Christ has died on the cross to accomplish my salvation. The freedom of the gospel means I need not worry about my eternal destiny because as Christ has been raised from the dead, so will I live again in God's heaven. The gospel sets the believer free from self-preoccupation.

How then do I live my life within the realm of such radical freedom? One option is to bask in God's love irresponsibly, as though Christ neither died nor was resurrected, as though Christ's spirit does not continue to breathe new life into us. Bonhoeffer called this particularly Lutheran temptation "cheap grace" and named it the deadly enemy of the church.[3] A second option is that we seek to avoid living in freedom by retreating into moralism and individualistic spirituality in the name of being "religious." Wandering in the wilderness of such radical freedom is so terrifying that we long for the fleshpots of legalism. This is the choice made by many "serious" Christians.

Martin Luther showed us a yet more excellent way (as did Jesus before him): "A Christian is a perfectly dutiful servant of all, subject to all." Or, in the words of Jesus, rooted deeply in Jewishness: "'Hear, O Israel: the Lord our God, the Lord is one; you shall love the Lord your God with all your heart, and with all your soul, and with all your mind, and with all your strength.' The second is this, 'You shall love your neighbor as yourself.'" (Mark 12:29-31). The love of God is inextricably intertwined with neighbor love. Christian freedom leads me inexorably to my neighbor.

The biblical imperative for justice

All Bible verses are not created equal. The core of Scripture we name by the doctrine of justification frees us for a second biblical trajectory that documents the imperative of neighbor love, beginning with the least, the most vulnerable. During the last three decades we have been summoned by "Third World" (more aptly described as "Two-Thirds World") Christians to awaken, as though arousing from deep slumber, to the massive biblical testimony witnessing to God's way of justice. Only our own level of material comfort and economic security as "First World" Christians could have made these texts invisible to us in the first place (much as we also unwittingly conspire to keep the hungry poor themselves out of sight).

The call for justice permeates Scripture's witness. God is revealed to Moses and the Israelites as a God of justice: "Then the LORD said: 'I have observed the misery of my people who are in Egypt; I have heard their cry on account of their taskmasters. Indeed, I know their sufferings, and I have come down to deliver them from the Egyptians, and to bring them up out of that land to a good and broad land, a land flowing with milk and honey . . .'" (Exod. 3:7-8; cf. also 2:23-25). The Lord hears the cries of the poor. In the promised land, there will be milk and honey, food for all.

One peculiar feature of the covenant law of Israel was its insistence on justice. Because God is righteous, God's law insisted that the covenant people be a people of righteousness toward the most vulnerable in its midst: "For the LORD your God is God of gods and Lord of lords, the great God, mighty and awesome, who is not partial and takes no bribe, who executes justice for the orphan and the widow, and who loves the strangers, providing them food and clothing" (Deut. 10:17-18; cf. also 24:17-22). God's law makes imperative the care for the least.

Leaders in Israel were expected to uphold a high standard of justice. Judges were expected to judge righteously. The king of Israel was expected to be the chief representative of God's justice: "So David reigned over all Israel; and David administered justice and equity to all his people" (2 Sam. 8:15). Likewise with regard to Solomon: "Blessed be the LORD your God, who has delighted in you and set you on the throne of Israel! Because the LORD loved Israel forever, he has made you king to execute justice and righteousness" (1 Kings 10:9). The Psalms resound with songs imploring God to make Israel's king just: "Give the king your justice, O God, and your righteousness to a king's son. May he judge your people with righteousness, and your poor with justice. . . . May he defend the cause of the poor of the people, give deliverance to the needy, and crush the oppressor" (Ps. 72:1-2, 4). The king is held to this standard because God is a God "who executes justice for the oppressed; who gives food to the hungry . . . " (Ps. 146:7). Jesus will draw from this royal tradition when he later announces the coming of God's kingdom.

Because the potential was (and is!) so great for a king to abuse power out of self-interest, there emerged at the same time as the office of king another figure, the prophet, to offer a check on the abuse of royal authority. Perhaps nowhere in Scripture does God's word on behalf of the poor and hungry sound more clearly than in the oracles of these prophets. "He has told you, O mortal, what is good; and what does the LORD require of you but to do justice, and to love kindness, and to walk humbly with your God?" (Micah 6:8). Furthermore, Micah declares: "Hear this, you rulers of the house of Jacob and chiefs of the house of Israel, who abhor justice and pervert all equity, who build Zion with blood and Jerusalem with wrong! Its rulers give judgment for a bribe, its priests teach for a price, its prophets give oracles for money; yet they lean upon the LORD and say, 'Surely the LORD is with us! No harm shall come upon us.' Therefore because of you Zion shall be plowed as a field; Jerusalem shall become a heap of ruins . . . " (Micah 3:9-12).

To give another example, Jeremiah spoke this word of God to the king of Judah: "Woe to him who builds his house by unrighteousness, and his upper rooms by injustice; who makes his neighbors work for nothing, and does not give them their wages; . . .Are you a king because you compete in cedar? Did not your father eat and drink and do justice and righteousness? Then it was well with him. He judged the cause of the poor and needy; then it was well. Is this not to know me? says the LORD" (Jer. 22:13, 15-16).

When the Messiah would come, this one would finally rule as a just king, representing God's righteousness: "A shoot shall come out from the stump of Jesse, and a branch shall grow out of his roots. The spirit of the LORD shall rest on him, the spirit of wisdom and understanding, the spirit of counsel and might, the spirit of knowledge and the fear of the LORD. His delight shall be in the fear of the LORD. He shall not judge by what his eyes see, or decide by what his ears hear; but with righteousness he shall judge the poor, and decide with equity for the meek of the earth; . . ." (Isa. 11:1-4). Consistently throughout the Hebrew Bible, God is revealed as the one who executes justice for the poor and hungry and who requires those yielding political, social, and economic power to uphold this standard. Kings and rulers must be held accountable for upholding their central responsibility of defending the cause of the poor and the hungry, all the vulnerable ones.

Kingdom of God, kingdom of justice

When Jesus began his public ministry, he established his mission squarely within this justice trajectory: "The Spirit of the Lord is upon me, because he has anointed me to bring good news to the poor. He has sent me to proclaim release to the captives and recovery of sight to the blind, to let the oppressed go free, to proclaim the year of the Lord's favor" (Luke 4:18-19). At the center of Jesus' message was the proclamation of the kingdom of God. "Kingdom" is a political term. Was it an accident that Jesus selected this guiding image for his ministry, a term which summons forth Israel's hope for a just and righteous king in the face of oppression?[4]

Jesus drew upon the Hebrew Scripture's testimony to Yahweh as a just king and defender of the poor as he shaped his central image of the *basileía toû theoû* (kingdom of God). The kingdom is not a place but the dynamic activity of God in the world now. "But if it is by the Spirit of God that I cast out demons, then the kingdom of God has come to you." (Matt. 12:28) Once Jesus was asked by the Pharisees when the kingdom of God was coming, and he answered, "The kingdom of God is not coming with things that can be observed; nor will they say, 'Look, here it is!' or 'There it is!' For, in fact, the kingdom of God is among you" (Luke 17:20-21).

The kingdom Jesus proclaimed brought near the reign of God to the people. Jesus' parables performed the kingdom[5], invoking the arrival of a near and merciful God (cf. the parables of the prodigal son and the good Samaritan). Jesus spoke pointedly on behalf of the hungry: "Blessed are you who are hungry now, for you will be filled . . . Woe to you who are full now, for you will be hungry" (Luke 6:21, 25). In the kingdom, the last will be first and the first last (Luke 13:30). In the parable of the rich fool, the rich man fails to see the folly of his ways and is unprepared for final judgment (Luke 12:16-21). Jesus summons the rich ruler to "sell all that you own and distribute the money to the poor" (Luke 18:22), a form of repentance he is unwilling to undergo (see Luke 18:18-25). "How hard it is for those who have wealth to enter the kingdom of God! Indeed, it is easier for a camel to go through the eye of a needle than for someone who is rich to enter the kingdom of God" (Luke 18:24-25). Zacchaeus demonstrates, however, that with God all things are possible, even the surrendering of one's possessions to the poor (Luke 19:1-10). Jesus declares in response to Zacchaeus' act of relinquishment: "Today salvation has come to this house" (Luke 19:9).

Moreover, by his actions Jesus instantiated the kingdom, that is, brought it into existence. Jesus healed the sick, cast forth demons, and miraculously fed hungry multitudes (Mark 6:30-44, 8:1-10). Jesus showed compassion on the crowds and challenged the disciples to respond in kind: "You give them something to eat" (Mark 6:37).

Jesus' own ministry was characterized particularly by unconventional table fellowship: "Why does he eat with tax collectors and sinners" (Mark 2:16)? The meals Jesus shared with others were a sign of the kingdom's dawning. He warned those who held banquets: "When you give a luncheon or a dinner, do not invite your friends or your brothers or your relatives or rich neighbors, in case they may invite you in return, and you would be repaid. But when you give a banquet, invite the poor, the crippled, the lame, and the blind" (Luke 14:12-13).

Jesus poignantly depicted the antikingdom through the parable of the rich man and Lazarus (Luke 16:19-31). In many ways the ministry of Jesus was lived out in battle with the powers of the demonic, the principalities and powers that threaten the destruction of life. Jesus engaged the powers of this world that accumulate control for themselves through their domination of the weak. Jesus' final battle with the principalities and powers led him to die on the cross.

Consistent with his concern for the manifestation of the kingdom at table, Jesus left his disciples a simple meal by which to remember him: "While they were eating, Jesus took a loaf of bread, and after blessing it he broke it, gave it to the disciples, and said, 'Take, eat; this is my body'" (Matt. 26:26). The eating of Jesus with tax collectors and sinners parallels the eating at the Lord's table: a welcome invitation to all, beginning with the outcast and sinners, the least. All are fed at the meal of Jesus.

The risen Jesus appeared to the disciples in the breaking of bread (Luke 24:30-31, cf. also John 21:12-13). The apostolic church of Acts is remembered for its generosity, flowing out from its table fellowship: "All who believed were together and had all things in common; they would sell their possessions and goods and distribute the proceeds to all, as any had need. Day by day, as they spent much time together in the temple, they broke bread at home and ate their food with glad and generous hearts . . ." (Acts 2:44-46). In this regard, it is important to recall the original reason the church began to collect an offering: as a collection for the poor. Likewise these early Christians remembered Jesus' words: ". . . for I was hungry and you gave me food . . . just as you did it to one of the least of these who are members of my family, you did it to me" (Matt. 25:35, 40).

Jesus, as demonstrated by his unconventional table fellowship and his concentration on the coming of the kingdom, stands directly in the center of the Jewish justice tradition. Concern for food and the hungry is not a distraction from the church's mission but belongs to the heart of Christian mission. Nowhere does this become more focused than in the prayer Jesus taught his disciples, known to us as the Lord's Prayer.

Questions for reflection and discussion

1. In what ways is the gospel of Jesus Christ radical and dangerous?
2. Bonhoeffer distinguishes between costly grace and cheap grace, calling the latter "the deadly enemy of the church." What did he mean? Do you agree? Why or why not?
3. Where are the hungry in your community?
4. Micah 6:8 reads: "And what does the Lord require of you but to do justice, and to love kindness, and to walk humbly with your God?" What does this mean to you as a Christian? To your congregation?
5. Who are the prophets of today?
6. How is the kingdom of God being manifested in our world today? In what ways does it have to do with political issues?

2

The Prayer Jesus Taught Us

"My neighbor's material needs are my spiritual needs."

∽ *Israel Salanter*[1]

Jesus on prayer

In the Gospels, Jesus says far more about the needs of the poor and oppressed than he does about prayer! This is a surprising claim. It is a discovery that could help to correct the potential imbalance between the church's concern for individual piety and its concern for social ministry. We will begin this chapter by examining this claim.

That Jesus prayed—and prayed regularly—is well documented in the gospels. When the evangelists mention Jesus at prayer, they usually do so by conjoining his praying with the performance of some extraordinary deed. [See, for example, Luke 3:21 (at his baptism), 5:16 (in conjunction with a healing), 6:12 (before calling the twelve disciples); Mark 6:46 (before walking on water); Luke 9:28-29 (at the transfiguration)]. The most moving and only lengthy account of Jesus at prayer occurs in the Garden of Gethsemane (Mark 14:32-42). Consistently, we see a direct relationship between Jesus' times of prayer and initiatives in active ministry. We can even say that for Jesus, prayer and action belong inseparably together. Sometimes we imagine Jesus' moments at prayer as retreats from activity. But we might even more assert that his times at prayer propel him into deeper and deeper engagement. Finally, at Gethsemane, Jesus is propelled to the cross. As Jesus immerses himself in devotion to his Father, he emerges into ministry on behalf of others. There exists a strong correlation between prayer and action in these texts.

Jesus has sharp words to say about how not to pray: not like hypocrites (Matt. 6:5-6), not heaping up words (Matt. 6:7), not like the Pharisees (Luke 18:10-11), not making long prayers (Mark 12:40), and in criticism of temple ritual (Mark 11:17). Notice how these criticisms of prayer typically point out the failure of one's prayer to conform with one's action. For example, hypocrisy is praying one thing and doing another.

Jesus offered some brief instructions regarding how to pray: alone in one's room (Matt. 6:6), for one's persecutors (Matt. 5:44), for laborers for the harvest (Matt. 9:38), to cast out an evil spirit (Mark 9:29), without losing heart (Luke 18:1), and following the example of the humble publican (Luke 18:10-11).

Somewhat shocking is the contrast between the followers of John and Jesus: "John's disciples, like the disciples of the Pharisees, frequently fast and pray, but your disciples eat and drink" (Luke 5:33). Interestingly, it's a charge Jesus did not deny. Other brief but significant references to prayer in the Gospels include Jesus' praying for the little children (Matt. 19:13), Jesus' promise that "whatever you ask for in prayer, believe that you have received it, and it will be yours" (Mark 11:24), and the reference to praying that the "end" not come in winter (Mark 13:18).

The Lord's Prayer and the things of this world

Given the brevity of Jesus' other instructions on prayer, it is no wonder that the Lord's Prayer has attained such a significant status in the Christian church. Here are words that Jesus, according to Luke, gave to his disciples in direct response to their request, "Lord, teach us to pray . . ." (Luke 11:1). Although there are good exegetical reasons to prefer Luke's terser version of the prayer as more original, we will attend to Matthew's account because of its greater similarity to the prayer offered in the church today:

> *Our Father in heaven,*
> *hallowed be your name.*
> *Your kingdom come.*
> *Your will be done,*
>   *on earth as it is in heaven.*
> *Give us this day our daily bread.*
> *And forgive us our debts,*
>   *as we also have forgiven our debtors.*
> *And do not bring us to the time of trial,*
>   *but rescue us from the evil one.* (Matt. 6:9-13)

Some commentators have asserted the deeply "spiritual" character of this prayer that Jesus taught his disciples. When I read the Lord's Prayer in light of the justice trajectory of the Hebrew Scriptures, alert to Jesus' own concern for the poor and oppressed, however, I am profoundly moved by how inexorably these petitions turn our attention away from heaven to our neighbor on earth. Directing our worship toward God in prayer leads us to pay heightened attention to our neighbor. In this way, the Lord's Prayer is nothing less than a justice prayer.

Jesus invited his disciples to address God as "Abba" ("Father"), a term of familiarity and intimacy. Yet the prayer makes clear the distinction of this father from all earthly fathers; this Father is "in heaven." The truth that God is in heaven, however, does not mean that God has nothing to do with earthly affairs. This particular heavenly Father compels us to pay attention to the things of this world.

The first petition accents the otherness of God: "hallowed be your name." With this petition we ask God to guard us from all idolatry. God's name participates in God's reality. As we do or do not respect God's name, so we express whether we set idols before God as priorities in our lives. This first petition is explained by Luther in the Large Catechism as referring both to "word or deed, speech or act":

> [God's name] is also profaned by an openly evil life and wicked works, when those who are called Christians and God's people are adulterers, drunkards, gluttons, jealous persons, and slanderers.[2]

Luther drew direct consequences from this petition for how we conduct ourselves in relationship to our neighbor. In fact, he does so consistently for the other petitions as well.

"Your kingdom come." As we have already seen, this petition is not so much a prayer for the end of the world as the request that the reign of God come over us even now. Regardless of what Jesus may have taught regarding an eschatological kingdom of God, what is distinctive about his proclamation of the kingdom is how it was coming near already in his words and deeds. When asked by disciples of John about the source of his authority, Jesus replied: "Go and tell John what you hear and see: the blind receive their sight, the lame walk, the lepers are cleansed, the deaf hear, the dead are raised, and the poor have good news brought to them" (Matt. 11:4-5). Signs of the kingdom all!

Notice how relentlessly the petitions of the Lord's Prayer move us into the dynamics of this world: "Your will be done, on earth as it is in heaven." Jesus does not teach us to pray for how things will be in heaven. God will take care of that. Rather, we are instructed to pray for the dawning of heavenly circumstances and heavenly relationships in the now. We are to pray that the kingdom come "also among us," to employ Luther's words. For wherever God's will is done, there reigns the kingdom.

The petition for daily bread (which will be taken up at greater length later in this chapter) is bracketed between these petitions for the inauguration of God's rule (and the fulfillment of God's will already on earth) and those about forgiveness and temptation. Does Jesus suddenly spiritualize the prayer by instructing the disciples to pray for forgiveness? Hardly! While we can scarcely even begin to think of forgiveness in economic terms, Jesus taught his disciples to pray for the forgiveness of "debts." Granted, Jesus surely would include a variety of offenses that shatter relationships under this petition. (See also Matt. 5:23-24.) But that this petition includes economic obligations is also clear. (cf. Matt. 5:25-26.)[3]

In doing so, Jesus was taking seriously provisions of the law regarding jubilee (cf. Lev. 25:8-12).[4] As Jesus had declared in his exposition of Isaiah's scroll in the synagogue of his hometown in Nazareth, "the year of the Lord's favor" (Luke 4:19) was fulfilled in his own ministry (Luke 4:14-21). In the kingdom of God all debts are settled—by being forgiven. Does this only refer to spiritual misdeeds? Does it not include the forgiveness of material debts as well? The connection between God's forgiveness of our debts and our forgiveness of the debts of others appears especially striking in this petition. The Lord's Prayer again leads us into and not away from the world with its broken relationships.

"And do not bring us to the time of trial, but rescue us from the evil one." Jesus did not get specific about the nature of the trials he had in mind. The range of situations in which one might face temptation is vast. Yet at the very heart of every temptation is the choice between trusting God's word or following the voice of another, the tempter. Such was the choice faced by Jesus when he was tempted in the wilderness, whether to trust God's promises or to follow temptation into idolatry (Luke 4:1-13). In this way the final petition of the Lord's

Prayer brings us full circle: whom do we trust, our Father in heaven or the tempter?

The Lord's Prayer in its entirety moves the believer from prayerful relationship with God toward relationship with the neighbor. Interestingly, nearly all of Luther's explanations of the petitions of the Lord's Prayer in some way direct us to our neighbor and the affairs of this world. Nowhere is this more poignant than in the petition for daily bread.

Give us this day our daily bread

"How much trouble there is now in the world simply on account of false coinage, yes, on account of daily exploitation and usury in public business, commerce, and labor on the part of those who wantonly oppress the poor and deprive them of their daily bread!"[5] Is this a quote from Karl Marx? No. Martin Luther. With these words Luther raised a critical voice against the disparity caused by injustice in his own society. Today the division between rich and poor, those with money and the hungry has reached epidemic proportions. The number of seriously hungry human beings was estimated at 800 million at the start of the new century. Nearly one billion human beings! Can we begin to fathom such a quantity of human need and suffering? It does not seem like so many to us because the hungry remain tidily tucked away in Nicaraguan villages and along back streets in Calcutta. Yet if you have eyes to see, the faces are plentiful to behold, not only in other countries but in your own backyard, county, and state. The largest percentage of the hungry is the most vulnerable: children and mothers.

"Give us . . . " We petition God for bread because ultimately all bread derives from God's hand. God is a bountiful provider. Christians have the conviction that God does provide enough bread for all. The problem is not bounty but distribution. Bread for the World reminds us that hunger could be stopped if and when we set it as our first priority.[6] But we as a culture live with an idolatrous faith, trusting not so much in God as in the beneficence of the market. We believe that when all individuals live competitively, each seeking his or her own self-interest, that this will work for the benefit of all. There is no empirical evidence for this belief. To the contrary, what we see as this belief spreads across the face of the planet is a growing disparity between the "haves" and "have nots"—800 million hungry neighbors. When we pray this petition, we acknowledge God is the provider and not the idolatrous invisible hand of the market.

" . . . this day . . . " The majority of the world's population has always lived hand to mouth. This was as true in the world of Jesus as it is for most of the world's population today. Jesus' prayer teaches us to live in gratitude for what God has provided and in dependence on God's new generosity each morning. But what about those who live in the shadow of war? What about refugees? What about those whose environment has been degraded? What about those who suffer drought, or flood, or tempest? What about those who have no work? What about the sick? The aged? The children? What about those whose wages are unjust? What about those whose natural resources have been exploited by others? What about those who grow plentiful crops but must sell them for export? From whence this day comes their bread? What invisible hand is reaching out to them?

" . . . our . . . " We pray not for "my" bread but for "our" bread. Who is this "our?" Me and my blood kin? Me and my race? Me and my congregation? Me and my nation? How many is the number of those with whom and for whom we pray for daily bread? When we pray for "our" bread, we pray for all of God's children to have bread. The "our" places us in solidarity with all of our neighbors, especially the hungry. We pray, "our," unselfishly for nearly one billion hungry, hidden neighbors.

" . . . daily . . . " We do not pray for excess bread. Luther was right to say that daily bread includes, "Everything in the necessities and nourishment of our bodies, such as food, drink, clothing, shoes, house, home, fields, livestock, money, property, an upright spouse, upright children, upright members of the household, upright and faithful rulers, good government, good weather, peace, health, decency, honor, good friends, faithful neighbors, and the like."[7] A danger arises, however, when my right to money and property comes into conflict with your right to bread. Our economic system is not designed for the immediate purpose of providing daily bread to feed the hungry but for the accumulation of "bread" in banks to feed capital investments. The availability of bread and other life necessities is supposed to occur miraculously as a consequence of this system. In the prayer Jesus teaches, he instructs us to return to the basics. The most basic of all human needs is for food and drink. Unless these are available for all, the rest of what we accumulate as daily bread is theft. For this reason, daily bread does require, in the words of Luther, "upright and faithful rulers" and "good government" which ensure bread for all.

" . . . bread . . . " By means of bread Jesus united matters of the flesh and matters of the spirit. Jesus fed both hungry multitudes and the hunger of the heart. Jesus demonstrated both the dawning of the kingdom as he sat at table with sinners and instituted the Lord's Supper for the forgiveness of sins. For Jesus there was no division between body and spirit. What Jesus has brought together, however, we have rent asunder. How do we reunite body and spirit as we come together to eat bread in Jesus' name?

The heresy of the Corinthian congregation was their failure to discern the body of Christ, i.e., the practice of a table fellowship at which the well-off ate their fill, neglecting the poor in their midst, but then presumed to come together at the Lord's

Supper as one happy family. Paul accused them of failing to discern the body, eating and drinking judgment against themselves (1 Cor. 11:17-34, esp. vs. 29). Paul preserved the unity of body and spirit in criticizing this abuse. Do we not fall under this condemnation when we spiritualize the blessings of Holy Communion without discerning that the body of Christ includes vast numbers who are physically hungry? How dare we come to the Lord's Table in a world where millions of Christian sisters and brothers lack daily bread? If we ask God in this petition for our own daily bread while we neglect the starving, it becomes tragically ironic that in the very next petition we beseech God for forgiveness. In our day, perhaps more than ever, these two petitions belong together.

As we gather around the Lord's Table week after week in our congregations at worship, we pray for the coming of God's kingdom—even that the kingdom may come to us. As we have seen, the kingdom for which we pray is one of justice—a kingdom in which the hungry are fed. Indeed through worship God in Christ is still at work to create this very kingdom in our midst through Word and Sacrament! The community which prays, "Give us this day our daily bread," and which has as its constitutive sacrament the breaking of bread in Jesus' name is by definition a community in service to the hungry. By virtue of partaking in the sacrament of bread, we become united with the one body of Christ among whose members are multitudes who are hungry. The question becomes not *if* but *how* we are going to share the bread on our tables with these hungry brothers and sisters.

Questions for reflection and discussion

1. How are prayer and action inseparable? What action does God expect of us as a result of our prayers?

2. "My neighbor's material needs are my spiritual needs." What does this mean? Do you agree? Why or why not?

3. Is the Lord's Prayer spiritual, political, or both?

4. In what ways can we not only share bread with the hungry but also "be" bread for them?

5. How are physical and spiritual hunger related?

6. "God's name participates in God's reality." Which names for God best describe God's reality for you?

7. We pray, "God's will be done." How do we discern God's will in a given situation?

8. "A danger arises when my right to money and property comes into conflict with your right to bread." What does this assertion have to do with our choices about lifestyle?

3

Hunger Imperatives!

"To leave men without food is a fault that no circumstance atten-uates; the distinction between the voluntary and the involuntary does not apply here."

    ∻ *Rabbi Yachanon*[1]

Hear the cries of the poor!

In preparation for this chapter, I invited several of Wartburg Seminary's international students to meet with me and respond to two basic questions: 1) What does hunger look like in your country? 2) What should the church be doing about it? Students from five countries, several of them pastors, gave responses—from Tanzania, Ethiopia, Namibia, El Salvador, and Papua New Guinea. This chapter begins with an account of what I heard from them.

In all five countries there exists deep concern for the problem of hunger, though the particular circumstances varied from country to country. From the outset we found it necessary to make a distinction between starvation and malnutrition. Starvation refers to the desperate hunger of masses of people for a defined period of time, due to natural disasters, such as hurricanes, earthquake, drought, or flood, but also exacerbated by official negligence or mismanagement. This is the present situation in North Korea and is spreading in eastern Africa. Malnutrition refers to the chronic shortage of food leading to the birth of premature babies, infant mortality, and greater susceptibility to life-threatening danger from various illnesses (e.g., malaria, flu, childhood diseases). Chronic malnutrition requires larger sums be spent on health care, diverts money away from education, limits individuals from fuller participation in economic activity, and diverts investment from other developmental priorities.

Anna and Benson spoke about the situation in Tanzania, where starvation is complicated whenever there is a period of drought. While in neighboring states there may be an excess of food, the two northern states have experienced starvation. Some people in the central part of the country have become so desperate that they sought to hand over their children to the care of others to keep them from starving. The problem has been complicated by inadequate social infrastructure and uneven distribution. One year's bumper crop was sold to obtain cash for payment of debts and purchase of goods. There is no satisfactory means to preserve last year's harvest. When one year's crop is not adequate, people begin to starve. Starvation means the schools close for three or four months. Without food, schools cannot open at any level, setting back the process of education. These regions are experiencing a tremendous setback that will affect them for years to come.

While starvation is a dramatic problem, the consequences of chronic malnutrition are even more devastating. In Tanzania, I was told that over half of the population is chronically malnourished. One pastor reported that, "You can see it in their eyes." The average lifespan is 51 years, the lowest in Africa. "Malnutrition is the most deeply rooted problem inhibiting the development of my country."

The hunger of church members has multiple effects on the ministry of the church. The pastor arrives at the church to preach and lead worship. The husbands are gone, searching for food. Families wait at home, anticipating the man's return. People avoid coming to church because of the expectation that they must bring food to share when they have none for their own children. When schools cut back on providing meals, families must themselves spend more to provide food for their own children who attend school. Malnutrition has multiple consequences for the church and its ministry. Contributions to the church are negatively impacted because people must spend more for food.

Solomon described the complex situation in Ethiopia, sharing photos of the faces of the hungry. He estimates that 20 to 25 percent of the 65 million people in the country are seriously malnourished, with that number on the increase. One fundamental issue magnifies the problem of hunger in his country: the people do not "own" their land. The government officially owns the land and there are many instances where those who have inhabited the land for generations have been summarily displaced. The policies of the government, complicated by corruption and bribery, undermine people's attachment to the land, leading those who live on the land to neglect its proper care, thus encouraging destructive practices like deforestation.

Government policies further exacerbate the plight of the hungry in that there are no government subsidies for farmers. In fact, the taxation of farmers, particularly during years of lean harvest, forces many to forfeit their land, driving them into permanent poverty. In some instances, farmers have had to contribute the food provisions needed for the sustenance of their own families in payment on taxes. Widespread fear of severe reprisals prevents the people from protesting unfair government policies.

In Ethiopia, the productivity of the land depends to a large degree on sufficient rainfall. Years of drought mean food shortages in many parts of the country. During periods of lack of rain, efficient and just methods of food distribution are crucial. The intervention of the international community during such times of crisis is imperative.

Most farming in Ethiopia continues to be done manually. This means that farmers depend greatly on animals, like oxen and cows, to assist in the work. Epidemic disease among farm animals is disastrous to farmers. Without an ox to help with the plowing and harvest, a farmer's yields are dramatically reduced. Farmers without farm animals tend to produce at only a subsistence level. They have no excess harvest to take to market and therefore gain no cash income with which they might purchase new animals to replace those lost to disease. Because there are few institutions that make small loans to farmers, it may take years to recover from a cycle of drought or the death of an animal. Some never do recover and these families succumb to chronic malnutrition, with no safety net to catch them when they fall.

In the western part of Ethiopia, farm production is significant. But also here are policies that lead to hunger. Businesses buy harvests at low prices. The government taxes at a high rate. Government companies sell fertilizers and other products at exorbitant prices. Food surpluses accumulate in the urban centers, but the price for food has now expanded to four times the cost paid to the farmers who grew it. By the time the food begins to be distributed to the outlying areas of the country, the quality has deteriorated and the prices have skyrocketed. Solomon summarized the situation by stating that hunger in Ethiopia is not just the result of the absence of rain but even more the absence of good and just government.

Daniel and Andries told of Namibia. Even after several years of independence from South Africa, there continues to be no food sufficiency. Namibia is still importing food from South Africa. While Namibia is a country rich in agriculture, the majority of the population is settled on "communal" lands with the best "commercial" land still occupied by a white minority. A key problem is thus land distribution. A related issue involves the exporting of crops and raw materials for the profit of the white minority, while the black majority must then pay high prices for manufactured imported goods.

The small farms of the black Namibians are greatly impacted by climate, with crop yields varying significantly from year to year. Irrigation is a major challenge, insofar as there are only two major rivers and Namibia is a dry country. There is also an urgent need for education in farming techniques and for more agricultural technology. Refugees place extra pressure on the food supply. Africa is a war-torn continent. When there is not enough food for your own people, there is even less to share with refugees from Angola or Zaire.

While there is no starvation in Namibia, malnutrition needs to be addressed by the government. Malnutrition means money spent for education and health programs is less effective than it could be, because hungry children are not physically or mentally prepared to learn. Malnutrition contributes to health problems (e.g., tuberculosis or infant diseases) and magnifies the devastating impact of AIDS.

Vilma described the present situation in El Salvador, where the problem of hunger has been intensified by twelve years of war, in which there were enormous violations of human rights. In 1992, the people voted for a government that would bring an end to the war. The war's end has in no way decreased the tension, however, between the needs of the poor majority of the population and the government that has represented the interests of the wealthy. The people are becoming poorer than ever. Vilma reported that sixty-seven percent of the population is poor, with 35 percent living in extreme poverty. The unemployment rate is over 50 percent. Most of the 45 percent of the population who live in rural areas lack basic services. In 1979, the illiteracy rate was 48 percent; now it is 58 percent. Only 6 percent have a college level education. The lack of education means that people are unqualified for most good paying jobs.

Major support for the economy comes from cash sent by family members living and working in other countries, like the

U.S., who send money back to their loved ones. People also survive by means of an informal economy. Other countries are investing in private enterprise in El Salvador, but not in the social infrastructure. For example, fast-food restaurants have been established throughout the country, but most of the people cannot afford to eat there. The banks support loans for large corporations but do not invest in small businesses. Polarization between rich and poor is increasing; the middle class is disappearing. Of those who have no economic means of support, many turn to crime. Most people were economically better off during the war than they are now.

Of the five countries represented, the most hopeful report in terms of hunger came from Kudud whose home is Papua New Guinea. Because of the isolation of the population, Papua New Guinea is a difficult country to study. The people live in three areas: most live in villages; others live and work in towns; still others have migrated to yet larger towns in order to "look for more," with many of these now staying in squatter settlements. Normally there are no serious hunger problems because the soil is rich. Occasionally, there have been periods of prolonged drought but the problem of hunger has been solved wherever people have shared with each other what they have. Supplies of food have been available. One concern is that of certain dietary deficiencies due to the nutritional uniformity of the foodstuffs grown (tubers, banana, taro, yams, cacao).

Even in Papua New Guinea, however, there are some disconcerting trends. Here too one observes increasing disparity between the wealthy and the poor. This has meant the implementation of policies that have negative impact on villages. Another danger is that of clear-cutting forests. If these trends continue, it will lead to an increase in hunger.

What should be the church's mission in the face of widespread hunger and poverty? There were several important answers given to this question by the international students. Where there is starvation, the church must provide not only material relief but also advocacy that the respective government respond to the crisis with responsibility. Where there is chronic malnutrition, the church needs to help provide social services—food, clean water supply, and medical support. Educational programs are urgently needed in agriculture, nutrition, and food preparation. Such education is especially necessary among the younger generation. Development projects, such as the Heifer project, have been very successful in some places, but nowhere sufficient to the need. Grassroots projects (e.g. providing bee hives, fish ponds, or poultry) offer not only material food support but also assist in providing needed education. Such projects are especially beneficial in developing self-reliance. Beyond these types of "in-kind" projects, however, people need cash generating income to purchase items that would otherwise be unavailable and to build economic security.

The students emphasized that the church has a key role to play not only in social service, but also in social advocacy. People need education in the causes of hunger and poverty. The trend toward private ownership leads to increased poverty as people are displaced from the land and lose their means of support. Unemployment is reaching crisis levels in many places. Commercialization creates consumer desires that clash with the need to provide basic human services—food, water, and housing. Governments must be called to accountability for the failure to provide basic necessities. The indebtedness of most of these countries means that they are forced to service the national debt rather than invest in the development of the services that meet the basic needs of the population. In its advocacy efforts, the church must work ecumenically in order to strengthen its voice. In the words of one student: "The church has the mission to denounce injustice and announce the good news of the kingdom of God."

Putting the problem of hunger in context by considering the unique situations in these five countries reveals that feeding the hungry is a complex challenge. While the biblical and theological imperatives about hunger are clear, in charting a particular course of action the church must also engage in detailed study of political, social, cultural, religious, and economic factors. A social statement on the economy by the church at large can contribute much to directing our efforts toward deeper understanding and more committed engagement in the midst of a complex reality, particularly on the macro-level. A social statement on the economy can provide direction for our advocacy efforts as a church. It can also offer an occasion for teaching in our synods and congregations. For implementation of specific programs, however, we depend on those who develop national, regional, and local strategies for implementation of particular projects that will directly meet the needs of the hungry. To this end we need the wisdom of those who direct our World Hunger Program and those who serve in global mission as they pay attention to the voices of those who live in a particular place. Finally, in developing strategies to stop hunger, we must listen to the hungry people themselves.

Combating hunger as a theological imperative

> There remains an experience of incomparable value. We have for once learned to see the great events of world history from below, from the perspective of the outcast, the suspects, the maltreated, the powerless, the oppressed, the reviled—in short from the perspective of those who suffer.[2] —Dietrich Bonhoeffer

Just as there were historical reasons for the emergence to prominence of the theme of justification in the 16th century, there are compelling historical reasons for the emergence of the theme of justice in the 21st century. What we need to learn is that prayer and neighbor love, justification and justice belong together. Justified sinners both acquire Christ's imputed right-eousness by faith and are made agents of God's justice by the power of the Spirit. The distinction that we make, for theological reasons, between justification and justice stems from the historical situation at the time of the Reformation and does not exist in the economy of God's Spirit. The Spirit that is at work in justification is the same One who makes us just, setting us free to live justly.

To pay attention to the cries of the poor in the world around us is to have our ecclesial business-as-usual interrupted as by a scream. How would you respond this very hour if even a few of the suffering hungry ones of this world stood as onlookers to your proceedings from the edges of your room? How would you be forced to think and act differently by virtue of being in the physical presence of even a single one who is starving? We could not continue per usual but would be forced to stop what we are doing and minister to that one. This is the very situation of the rich man and Lazarus (Luke 16:19-31). Lazarus sits right outside our room, out of sight and out of mind. Therefore we proceed with our, yes, important agendas, leaving Lazarus to fend for himself. Lazarus exists only at the periphery of consciousness. We awaken to his plight on global or inner city immersion experiences but the enormity of the problem overwhelms us and we quickly find ways to shelter ourselves from the stark reality of almost a billion hungry Lazaruses.

The evil of hunger deserves urgent attention from the church. The pervasiveness of hunger—800 million hungry human beings—forces us to think in terms of numbers that boggle the imagination. If we rightly stand aghast at a system that manufactured the holocaust of six million Jews, how is it we fail to be scandalized by the death today of 30,000 children from hunger-related causes? Phil Hefner writes:

> I believe that the destructiveness and suffering heaped upon persons by economic and social class divisions in the United States may well be known in the next century as our own "confessing church" problem. In Germany under Hitler, the churches brought disgrace upon themselves for their failure to recognize the anti-Jewish policies of the society and make efforts to counter them. The Confessing Church emerged from a remnant of the churches and did work underground against Hitler's policies and did attempt to serve the needs of the Jews. Even today, the mainstream churches bear the stigma of their failure, and the Confessing Church stands as a courageous attempt to be the authentic church under Hitler. Thirty years from now we may well find our churches falling under a similar judgment of history. Millions of Americans are becoming increasingly poor and disenfranchised. What record of protest and ministry have our churches presented in the face of this trend?[3]

As members of a church, how can we theologically and morally tolerate a status quo in which the reality of 800 million malnourished human beings is considered "normal" and "acceptable"?

As the church takes seriously its social teaching on economic life, we have many alternatives as to how we may choose to address the complexity of the questions that face us.[4] In our capacity as church, however, given the immensity of human suffering due to hunger and given the clarity of the biblical witness concerning justice for the poor, we have as our first obligation to speak boldly and consistently about the need to attend first to the needs of the hungry and to advocate for systemic change to ensure priority is given to their needs. Other institutions can and will assume other postures with regard to what makes for good economics. Whatever else we say as a church about the economy, our first and last word must be about God's concern for those hungry children of God whose lives rapidly become invisible when talk turns to economic theory. In my opinion, this is the most faithful and truly necessary thing the church has to offer to a public discussion of economic matters: in the economy of God, the needs of all people are given consideration, beginning with the least.

Dr. Martin Luther King, Jr. preached these words in his sermon, "A Knock at Midnight":

> The church must be reminded that it is not the master or the servant of the state, but rather the conscience of the state. It must be the guide and critic of the state, and never its tool. If the church does not recapture its prophetic zeal, it will become an irrelevant social club without moral or spiritual authority. If the church does not participate in the struggle for peace and economic and racial justice, it will forfeit the loyalty of millions and cause men everywhere to say that it has atrophied its will. But if the church will free itself from the shackles of a deadening status quo, and, recovering its great historic mission, will speak and act fearlessly and insistently in terms of justice and peace, it will enkindle the imagination of mankind and fire the souls of men, imbuing them with a glowing and ardent love for truth, justice, and peace.[5]

As we continue to ponder the future of ecumenical relationships with those churches with whom we are in full communion and those others with whom we have strong relationships, here is a task worthy of our time and effort: to cooperatively and in unity rejoin our efforts both in terms of immediate relief of human suffering and in advocacy for structural change on behalf of the hungry. While the record of ecumenical cooperation in social ministry for the hungry has been strong, the hour has come for giving even more central prominence to these efforts as church bodies. Such a witness would give visibility to the tangible difference made by ecumenical cooperation and provide a worthy outlet for new expressions of common cause. Feeding the hungry is an arena where ecumenical cooperation in mission is not a slogan but achieves visible and tangible results.

To propose combating hunger as a matter of *status confessionis*, as will be elaborated in the next chapter, means that we must turn from whatever else we are doing and respond to the silent screams of the hungry. Already in Lutheran history, an ethical use of *status confessionis* was declared by the Lutheran World Federation in 1977 as the moment for ending apartheid in South Africa found its *kairos* ("opportune moment"). Apartheid was named as an evil of monstrous proportions. For the church to justify, or even tolerate, a system that produced a policy of apartheid was tantamount to heresy. The problem of hunger may be equally urgent, and even more insidious because of the invisibility of the poor from our daily routines.

Questions for reflection and discussion

1. "To leave men without food is a fault that no circumstance attenuates: the distinction between the voluntary and the involuntary does not apply here." Do you agree or disagree with this claim? Why or why not?

2. This chapter began with two questions: 1) What does hunger look like in your country? 2) What should the church be doing? How would you answer these questions about the United States and the community in which you live?

3. In what ways is hunger influenced by racism? Sexism? What other factors influence hunger?

4. The international students interviewed named stark disparity between rich and poor in their countries. In what ways does that disparity exist where you live?

5. "The church has the mission to denounce injustice and announce the good news of the kingdom of God." Does your congregation see this as its mission? If so, how are you accomplishing it?

6. You may have heard the saying, "Live simply, so that others may simply live." What does this mean? Discuss the biblical basis for the following saying: "Live justly, so that others may just live."

7. How would you respond if even a few of the suffering hungry ones stood as onlookers to your evening meal from the edges of the room?

8. As baptized members of the church, how can we theologically and morally tolerate a status quo in which the reality of nearly one billion malnourished human beings is considered "normal" and "acceptable"?

4

Stopping Hunger: A Matter of *Status Confessionis*[1]

What would it take to provoke the church of Jesus Christ to repentance for failing to feed Christ incarnate in the hungry neighbor (Matt. 25:42)?

The piling up of statistics?[2] Over 800 million people in this world are chronically malnourished, 153 million of them are under the age of five. Thirteen million children in the United States under the age of eighteen are hungry. 10.4 percent of the U.S. population either experience hunger or are at risk of hunger. How have our minds become so dulled that such statistics become innocuous?

The piling up of dead bodies? Thirty thousand children die each day of hunger-related causes. The risk of dying from a given disease is doubled for *mildly* malnourished children, and tripled for those *moderately* malnourished. Who can measure the risks for those millions who are *chronically* malnourished? One child under the age of five dies every five seconds. If it takes you ten minutes to read this chapter, sixty children will die of hunger-related causes during that time. How have our hearts become so hardened that we do not feel outrage?

The piling up of Bible verses? Ronald Sider has performed a genuine service by compiling an anthology of Scripture passages pertaining to the matter of social justice. The edited texts, entitled *Cry Justice: The Bible on Hunger and Poverty*, total no less than 188 pages.[3] The very core of the Christian Bible shouts out compassion and justice for the hungry. Reference was made earlier to the parable of the Great Judgment in

Matthew 25, where the wicked are cast into the eternal fire for failing to minister to Christ in the form of the hungry neighbor. The biblical witness testifying to the imperative of feeding the hungry is clear, unambiguous, and massive. How have our eyes become so blinded that we can read God's Word and not see the starving neighbors to whom it refers?

Another parable, the rich man and Lazarus, in itself ought to suffice to summon the church to repentance for a world of hungry neighbors. Lazarus sits at the very gate of the rich man. Yet poor Lazarus remains invisible. And the rich man feasts sumptuously every day. After both are dead, the rich man is tormented in Hades and asks Abraham to summon Lazarus to minister to his need. This request denied, the rich man begs Abraham to send Lazarus to warn his living relatives.

> Abraham replied, "They have Moses and the prophets; they should listen to them." He said, "No, father Abraham; but if someone goes to them from the dead, they will repent." He said to him, "If they do not listen to Moses and the prophets, neither will they be convinced even if someone rises from the dead." (Luke 16:29-31)

Neither have we been convinced by the raising of Jesus from the dead.

How many North American Christians, particularly educators, have already had opportunity to travel to those countries where most of the people are poor? Globalization has been a predominant motif in recent theological education. An experience in Mexico typifies my schooling in world hunger. Recall the visit I made to a *campesino* named Manuel in a village near Cuernavaca (see Introduction). Naturally, we began by asking him something about his family. He spoke simply, matter-of-factly: "I have ten children. Seven you see here. Three of them died as babies." They died from the diseases of malnutrition. Manuel's words have been echoed by other parents' voices in every poor country I have visited. Children die daily, as a matter of course, for lack of basic nutrition. To Manuel and thousands like him, the death of Lazarus is the death of a child, a regular occurrence.

In the last decades a cry arose from the poor of the earth through the voices of liberation theologians. Their theology originates from the standpoint of the world's poor. Never before has a theology so consistently addressed both God's Word and the situation of the world's marginal people. Never before has a theology raised such a challenge to those who dare to write thick theological books but ignore the requisites of justice. For presuming, on scriptural grounds, to argue God's preferential option for the poor, liberation theology has been criticized as Marxist and slandered unmercifully. Its impact has been neutralized and the cry of the poor has been effectively muffled. But this in no way alters the facts of the case: the God of the Christian Bible is a God who is revealed as one who shows preferential concern for the hungry.

What theological resources are available to awaken the church from its coma, to inspire response to the crisis of its hungry neighbors? As I search for an answer to this question, I submit a provocative proposal: that stopping hunger attain the priority of a matter of *status confessionis*, a concern of utmost confessional significance. Although the reality of hunger in our world is pandemic and therefore insidious, the church of Jesus Christ must more than ever before raise a clarion call: existing circumstances are intolerable and feeding the hungry must become a component of core Christian identity. Simply to lament the plight of the hungry is insufficient. The church must be summoned to respond to the hungry neighbor as to Jesus Christ himself. In the words of St. Rose of Lima: "When we serve the poor and the sick, we serve Jesus. We must not fail to help our neighbors, because in them we serve Jesus."[4] At stake is the integrity of the gospel itself and the working out of our own salvation (See Phil. 2:12).

Defining *status confessionis*

Although arising in a German context, the Latin term, *status confessionis*, does not appear as such in the Lutheran confessional writings. The idea derives from the Solid Declaration (paragraph 10, 8-10) of the Formula of Concord:

> We also believe, teach and confess that in a time when confession is necessary, as when the enemies of God's Word want to suppress the pure teaching of the holy gospel, the entire community of God, indeed, every Christian, especially servants of the Word as leaders of the community of God, are obligated according to God's Word to confess true teaching and everything that pertains to the whole of religion freely and publicly. They are to do so not only with words but also in actions and deeds. In such a time they shall not yield to the opponents even in indifferent matters, nor shall they permit the imposition of such adiaphora by opponents who use violence or chicanery in such a way that undermines true worship of God or that introduces or confirms idolatry.[5]

This paragraph defines circumstances in which faithfulness to God's Word requires giving confessional status to a secondary issue (*adiaphoron*) for the sake of defending the gospel. Such a "time when confession is necessary" summons all Christians "to confess true teaching and everything that pertains to the whole of religion freely and publicly. They are to do so not only with words but also in actions and deeds." The "true teaching" to which we here appeal is the biblical teaching regarding compassion and justice for people in physical need.

The history of interpretation and application of the concept *status confessionis* has been of two types. A *restrictive* interpretation applies only when the very identity of the church is temporarily threatened, when a persecution that imposes false teaching would force it into idolatry and heresy. It thus refers to very particular conflicts between church and state. Such times for confessing arose in the political strife of the Reformation period and in Nazi Germany with the attempt to apply the Aryan paragraph to the church, a law that sought to remove from office all pastors of Jewish descent. Dietrich Bonhoeffer, early in the church struggle, saw resistance to Nazi interference in the affairs of the church as such a matter of *status confessionis*. A restrictive interpretation greatly minimizes the number of occasions in which a *status confessionis* could apply.

A second, *ethical* interpretation of *status confessionis* broadens the range of instances where the church might choose to declare an issue to be of confessional stature. Karl Barth took this position, expanding the scope of *status confessionis* beyond the church struggle per se into general opposition to the Hitler regime. He opposed Nazi rule and policies as a matter of Christian conscience and appealed to others to do likewise as part of their fundamental confession of faith. The movement countering the influence and leadership of the state church (the "German Christians") came to be known as the *Confessing* Church.

In 1968 W. A. Visser't Hooft, General Secretary of the World Council of Churches from its foundation in 1948 until 1966, declared: "It must become clear that church members who deny in fact their responsibility for the needy in any part of the world are just as much guilty of heresy as those who deny this or that article of the faith."[6] The concept of "ethical heresy" informs this second interpretation of *status confessionis*.

Meeting at Dar es Salaam in 1977, delegates to the Lutheran World Federation's Sixth Assembly issued this summons to member churches:

> We especially appeal to our white member churches in Southern Africa to recognize that the situation in Southern Africa constitutes a *status confessionis*. This means that, on the basis of faith and in order to manifest the unity of the church, churches would publicly and unequivocally reject the existing apartheid system.[7]

Other appeals seeking to elevate a contemporary concern to the level of *status confessionis* have been made with reference to the rejection of nuclear weapons (by church "brotherhoods" in Germany during the late 1950s and 60s and the Executive Board of the Reformed Alliance in Germany in 1982) and in opposition to demythologizing (in Germany during the 1960s).[8] More recently the issue has been raised through an appeal to *kairos*—the proposal that *now* is the opportune time to confess and act—with documents arising from South Africa, Central America, the United States, and a coalition with representatives from several nations.[9] George Hunsinger has argued (in 1985) that the political and theological issues facing the church in America (human rights violations, U.S. policy in the Third World, nuclear arms, racism) require a confessing church today,[10] while Ulrich Duchrow has proposed (in 1986) that the transformation of the world economic system deserves attention as an issue for a contemporary confessing church movement.[11]

A pitfall of declaring contemporary ethical issues occasions for a confessing church and reasons for declaring *status confessionis* is the endless list of special interests that might be proposed. The debate surrounding the adoption of the LWF resolution regarding apartheid illustrates the difficulty of attaining consensus. Any proposal to adopt a specific concern as a matter of *status confessionis* must be thoroughly studied and discussed. Yet a particular issue becomes *de facto*, a matter of utmost confessional concern not when a church body adopts a resolution but when a consensus emerges among Christian people that this cause is imperative for the integrity of the faith itself. Adopting confessional status for ending hunger is a dramatic strategy—a peculiar recourse for elevating the discussion to the priority it deserves. Here is an issue of utmost urgency, literally a matter of life and death.

The imperative to stop hunger transcends denominational divisions. The testimony of the Scriptures regarding God's defense of the poor and hungry is so strong that it belongs to the *sensus fidei* ("sense of faith") of the entire catholic church (cf. *Lumen Gentium* 12). The time has come for all churches to acknowledge both their biblical heritage and the scandal of hunger in the contemporary world. A *kairotic* ecumenical consensus could consolidate efforts to eliminate hunger in the 21st century. Such a shared *consensus fidelium* ("concensus of the faithful") of the ecumenical church would attain results far beyond any individual denomination's.

At the core of the Christian faith

How then does commitment to ending hunger belong to the core convictions of the Christian faith? The hub of 16th-century theology was the question: what is necessary for salvation? Opposing any claim to righteousness by works, the evangelical parties confessed salvation by grace through faith for Christ's sake. Our proposal to adopt concern for the hungry as a matter of *status confessionis* ought not be considered a condition placed on the gospel. Salvation has been won by Christ's death and resurrection and by this alone. However, given the magnitude of starvation at the beginning of the 21st century and the biblical mandate to feed the hungry, this proposal would establish Christian commitment toward elimination of hunger as the highest priority in our response to God's grace. To be a Christian in a world of massive hunger is to minister "not only with words but also in actions and deeds" to feed hungry people. We do so because the Bible is so clear and overwhelming in its witness, understanding that we will be judged on the basis of our response to the hungry neighbor.

To this end, a comfortable church must awaken from its sloth into compassionate action. Sloth is the deadly sin that seduces the church into complacency by cheapening God's grace. It is our sloth that steals from us any sense of urgency in responding to the needs of our hungry neighbors, replacing urgency with a sense of futility. We become indifferent, apathetic, spiritually dead. In the case of starving people, the sloth of the comfortable is literally a deadly sin for those who daily perish. Though we are saved by grace, we are truly to be judged by our works. How severe will be that judgment if we neglect to feed our hungry neighbor! The response to the needs of the poor has consequences both for their salvation and ours: their physical condition is inextricably linked to our spiritual wholeness. To disregard a world of hungry neighbors steals from our own humanity. James pleads:

> What good is it, my brothers and sisters, if you say you have faith but do not have works? Can faith save you? If a brother or sister is naked and lacks daily food, and one of you says to them, "Go in peace; keep warm and eat your fill," and yet you do not supply their bodily needs, what is the good of that? So faith by itself, if it has no works, is dead. (James 2:14-17)

Some scholars describe this passage as an intentional polemic against the consequences of an antinomian interpretation of Paul's teaching on justification. Salvation by grace through faith can become a self-satisfying mind game, detached from the experience of human suffering. Grace so cheapened is no grace at all. A fat church, basking in God's grace while the hungry starve, needs the shock therapy of James.

But it is one thing to take care of a brother or sister who confronts you in the starkness of their nakedness or hunger and another altogether if you cannot see them at all. This was the sin of the church in Corinth. When this church gathered to eat the Lord's Supper, it divided into factions. At the meal preceding the sharing of the loaf and cup, some ate their fill (one would assume from their own provisions) while others went hungry. Although gathered in the same place, those with plenty took no account of those without. Then all presumed to come together to the Lord's Supper.

Paul judges the Corinthians to be guilty of profaning the body and blood of Christ. He writes:

> Whoever, therefore, eats the bread or drinks the cup of the Lord in an unworthy manner will be answerable for the body and blood of the Lord. Examine yourselves, and only then eat of the bread and drink of the cup. For all who eat and drink without discerning the body, eat and drink judgment against themselves. (1 Cor. 11:27-29)

We are the Corinthians, guilty of failing to discern the body of Christ when we eat and drink, neither perceiving the hunger of those around us nor sharing our provisions. Our culpability is especially scandalous when the hungry include so many baptized brothers and sisters in Christ. To eat the Lord's Supper without commitment to feed the hungry is to eat and drink judgment upon ourselves.

To consider stopping hunger as a matter of *status confessionis* entails the belief that there is indeed enough food for all.

Jesus' frequently cited words, "For you always have the poor with you . . . " must cease to serve as a rationale justifying a world of hungry neighbors. Instead we must listen to the rest of this saying, " . . . and you can show kindness to them whenever you wish," as a summons to action (Mark 14:7). Just as it was once inconceivable that there be a world without slavery or a society where men and women are equal, so today we can scarcely imagine a world where all people have food to eat. Yet such a world would be realizable if there were but the will to put feeding the hungry at the top of our agenda. The final issue is not insufficient resources but their just distribution. Were we to attain fairness of food distribution, this would still not be the kingdom of God. But it would be a welcome anticipation thereof.

Practical implications

What would ending hunger as matter of *status confessionis* mean in practical terms? For individual Christians, it would mean an intentional ordering of lifestyle to include acts of charity and advocacy for the poor. One would be challenged to examine all one's spending habits according to their impact on hungry people. In the year 2000 Lutherans gave an average of only $3.00 per member per year to denominational hunger programs. Such a giving level indicates vast ignorance (also indifference?) regarding the urgency of the problem. Charitable giving to hunger programs would become as normal as giving to current operating expenses of a congregation. Members would routinely volunteer to work in local soup kitchens and food pantries, providing both material assistance and direct personal connection to those who are poor.

In such a church, it would become standard procedure for members to write letters and otherwise communicate to members of Congress regarding bills that affect the welfare of the hungry. Participation in an organization like Bread for the World would be viewed as a basic expression of Christian concern. All legislation would be first evaluated for its impact on marginal people rather than on the criterion of self-interest. In a church where stopping hunger were a matter of *status confessionis*, members would set aside partisan political commitments and examine all political questions from the perspective of the hungry. Whether Democrat or Republican in origin, all economic and political strategies would be evaluated on the basis of their effectiveness in alleviating hunger.

In a church committed to ending hunger, the increased amounts of money available would multiply relief efforts and dramatically increase the number and types of developmental projects. Record numbers of members would volunteer to work in domestic and international projects that aim to improve the standard of living for the poor. In terms of advocacy, a church confessionally committed to eliminating hunger would continually educate members on the structural barriers impeding the availability of food for all and raise a collective voice for social structures which serve those most in need. The church would redouble efforts to sustain interest in stopping hunger over the long haul, transcending the sporadic attention given to immediate relief during times of famine or disaster. Bishops and pastors would so integrate concern for the hungry into their teaching that awareness of the need would consistently permeate our consciences. In short, the hunger program of the church would be lifted up from its status as one concern among many and be privileged among the pressing issues of Christian conscience today. Faithful response to the gospel at the beginning of the 21st century would require action to eliminate hunger. In implementing the Evangelical Lutheran Church in America's social statement on the economy, alleviating hunger would deserve the highest priority as that economic issue about which the church must raise its voice.

Is a proposal to declare stopping hunger a matter of *status confessionis* too utopian to take seriously? Does it hopelessly confuse law and gospel? Many objections can be raised. If not this, what measures do you propose that can summon the church to eliminating this great cause for scandal?

Questions for reflection and discussion

1. What does the phrase "separation of church and state" mean? Should the church speak out on political issues?

2. What are the responsibilities of church members with regard to the hungry?

3. "When the church is silent, it supports the *status quo*." What does this statement mean? Do you agree? Why or why not?

4. What is the relationship between being saved by God's grace and being judged by God according to our works?

5. What does it mean to "discern"? How do we "discern" the body of Christ in relationship to the hungry?

6. What belongs to the core commitments of your own confession of Christian faith? Where do the needs of the hungry fit in?

7. What are some ways in which your congregation can raise its voice and organize action on behalf of the hungry?

8. In what ways should the church be involved in advocacy efforts to help the hungry?

5

Ending Hunger:
A Real Possibility

"You give them something to eat."

― *Jesus of Nazareth, Luke 9:13*

Ending hunger is a real possibility. This is no utopian dream. One insidious myth that prevents churches and people of good will from mobilizing the forces necessary to eliminate hunger is the conviction that the goal is unattainable. Yet organizations like Bread for the World and the Institute for Food and Development Policy (FoodFirst), groups that are realistic in their assessment of world food policies, argue persuasively that what is lacking is not sufficient food supply but rather the political will.

The world currently produces enough grain to provide a diet of 3500 calories a day for every human being on the planet.[1] This does not include other common foodstuffs such as vegetables, fruit, beans, nuts, fish, or grass-fed livestock. Were the calculation to include all sources of food, the amount available would escalate to 4.3 pounds per person per day, enough to make us fat! We live in a food abundant world, not in a world where food is scarce. This means that the primary issues in ending hunger have to do, first, with making it a priority in our public policy and, second, insisting on just food distribution.

Food is a human right

How we think about access to food makes a tremendous difference. Currently what exists in the global economy is a system whereby *food is primarily understood as an industry*. The evolution of the food industry in the last decade has exacted a heavy price on, among other things, the viability of the family farm. Food is a for-profit business in which corporations largely control the production (e.g., land, seeds, fertilizers, pesticides, machinery), processing (e.g., purchase, shipping, refinement, packaging), and distribution (e.g., marketing, delivery, sales, advertising) of food throughout the world. Within this system, food is understood as a commodity that is for sale according to a calculus of calories, cost, and profit margin.

In this, as in any other industry, it is advantageous to consider the commodity in question to be scarce, rather than plentiful. Controlling the supply is a key element in the market economy, including mechanisms that create the appearance of scarcity. Government regulates this industry to a certain extent, particularly to guarantee the safety of what we eat. Charitable organizations organize efforts to provide food to the world's poorest people, particularly during times of famine. But in their respective roles, both government and charitable organizations operate within the fundamental framework that understands food primarily as a business enterprise.

While there are many benefits that accrue from the business of food-for-profit, such as the efficiency of mass production and the incredible variety in consumer selection, a fundamental moral problem challenges the current system: over 800 million human beings are currently chronically malnourished. The agony of this reality requires at least a structural adjustment in the world food system as presently constituted, if not a fundamental paradigm shift in our collective understanding of the human right to food.

How might we achieve a fundamental shift from the current paradigm of understanding food primarily in terms of an industry to one where we give priority to access to *food as a basic human right?* The foundation for the moral corrective was already laid by the United Nations on December 10, 1948 when the UN General Assembly adopted Article 25 of the Universal Declaration of Human Rights:

> Everyone has the right to a standard of living adequate for the health and well-being of himself and of his family, including food, clothing, housing, and medical care and necessary social services, and the right to security in the event of unemployment, sickness, disability, widowhood, old age or other lack of livelihood in circumstances beyond his control.[2]

At the first World Food Conference in 1974, the human right to food was affirmed in an even more pointed way when the assembly declared: "Every man, woman, and child has the inalienable right to be free from hunger," adding that "no child will go to bed hungry, that no family will fear for its next day's bread, and that no human being's future and capacities will be stunted from malnutrition."[3] According to these human rights provisions, governments do not have an obligation to provide food for their entire population; they do, however, have a responsibility to enact measures that guarantee that no one goes without food. The role of government in a system that defends access to food as a human right would provide legal structures that modified the existing food industry to safeguard a minimum dietary threshold for each citizen, beginning with the needs of those most vulnerable, women and children.

The affirmation of a basic human right to food has yet to be taken seriously by many governments throughout the world. In the United States, the Senate passed The Right-to-Food resolution on September 16, 1976. The U.S. House of Representatives version of the resolution, which passed on September 21, 1976, reads:

Resolved by the House of Representatives (the Senate concurring), that it is the sense of the Congress that:

the United States reaffirms the right of every person in this country and throughout the world to food and a nutritionally adequate diet; and

the need to combat hunger shall be a fundamental point of reference in the formulation and implementation of United States policy in all areas which bear on hunger including international trade, monetary arrangements, and foreign assistance; and

in the United States, we should seek to improve food assistance programs for all those who are in need, to ensure that all eligible recipients have the opportunity to receive a nutritionally adequate diet, and to reduce unemployment and ensure a level of economic decency for everyone; and

the United States should emphasize and expand it's assistance for self-help development among the world's poorest people, especially in countries seriously affected by hunger and malnutrition, with particular emphasis on increasing food production and encouraging more equitable patterns of food distribution and economic growth; and such assistance, in order to be effective, should be coordinated with expanded efforts by international organizations, donor nations, and the recipient countries to provide a nutritionally adequate diet for all.

(As passed by the U.S. Senate (S. Con. Res. 138) on September 16, 1976.)[4]

Taken seriously, the substance of this legislation provides the agenda for the paradigm shift necessary for making food, above all else, a human right. Like other nations, however, the United States has yet to enact policies that are consistent with the priorities set forth in this admirable legislation. One role for a church that takes seriously the ending of hunger as a matter of *status confessionis* would be to insist that each respective government implement both domestic and international policies consistent with the intent of such Right-to-Food legislation.

What would be the cost of ending hunger in our world? According to United Nations sources cited by Bread for the World, the estimated cost in 1998 of providing basic nutrition, health care, education, water, and sanitation to all the world's people was $40 billion a year.[5] The U.S. Agency for International Development also in 1998 estimated that the cost of reducing world hunger by half in the next fifteen years would cost a total of $45 billion. The yearly cost to the nations of the world would be only $3 billion. If the cost of eliminating hunger were now to be as high as $50 billion per year, this still would be a very attainable goal, should this become a political priority for the international community. In such an effort, "a fair share for the U.S. government might be $5 billion. That's less than one-half of 1 percent of the federal budget. People in the United States spend $8 billion each year on cosmetics."[6] Compared to the amounts expended for military and other national security measures, the amount needed to provide food security for the world's people is very modest. What kind of international security might be attained were the leading nations of the world to make food sufficiency an indispensable prerequisite in their diplomacy?

While our entry into matters of politics necessitated the preceding description of access to food as a human right, Christians have an even more compelling reason for insisting on the elimination of world hunger: ultimately food is a gift of God to be shared freely and generously with those in need.[7] Food is not an optional commodity that only consumers of means should have the ability to purchase. God desires that all people flourish, which at the bare minimum includes an adequate diet, regardless of one's ability to buy. God created food for the sake of human delight, sustenance, and sharing. Thus food is not only a necessity, but even more a gift to be enjoyed and shared. What Christians view in theological terms is best translated into the language of human rights in the non-Christian province of politics and economics.

Equitable food distribution: The church's advocacy role

Not only does the church have a critical responsibility in establishing that there is enough food for all and that minimum food sufficiency is a human right. The church also has a critical role to play in educating about the causes of hunger and engaging in advocacy to address those causes.[8] In this context it is important to distinguish between the efforts of the church in the area of "social service" (providing direct relief in feeding those who are hungry) and the role of the church in "social advocacy." Advocacy efforts seek to change the political and economic structures that leave people hungry in the first place.

Advocacy efforts on the part of the church in changing the political and economic systems that leave 800 million people hungry will be most effective when conducted with ecumenical and global partners. The Lutheran World Federation supports in principle the responsibility of the church to engage in advocacy "to redress or lessen the unjust effects of economic globalization through advocacy work to hold institutions accountable for their God-given responsibilities."[9] Particular sensitivity needs to be given to the nature of North-South partnerships. "Although it is especially churches in the global North who have closer access to the decision-makers of transnational corporations, it is important that this advocacy work be linked with those who are affected in specific, harmful ways by corporate practices in the global South."[10] It is particularly in the churches of the South that the call for ending hunger resounds most clearly.

In order for the church to engage effectively in its role as advocate for ending hunger, it will need to develop a complex analysis of the causes of hunger and be vigilant in formulating a strategy that addresses this complexity. The following section identifies *ten key factors* that need to be incorporated into a comprehensive plan for ending world hunger.[11]

Equalizing the benefits of economic globalization.[12] While the trickle down effect of a global economy has meant the difference between survival and starvation for many, the incredible gap between the rich and poor continues to widen in an increasingly global economy. While the richest one-fifth in the world control 85% of the world Gross National Product (GNP) and the middle three-fifths are allotted 14% of the world GNP, the poorest one-fifth share only 1% of the world GNP.[13] Such disparity is finally a major cause of global instability and insecurity.

Revising the policies of the World Bank and International Monetary Fund according to the criteria of their impact on the poorest of the poor. This will require a greater level of consultation between these influential monetary institutions and the people at the grass roots who are most affected by the measures they impose, such as in times of "structural adjustment." Much of the burden of heavily indebted nations is borne by the most marginal portion of the population. There is precedent for forgiveness of debt where the prospect for repayment is either impossible or where the consequences for the poor are simply intolerable. This later consideration is particularly relevant for several African countries.

Refocusing U.S. foreign aid on humanitarian and development purposes. Contrary to the common impression, the United States ranks last among the top twenty industrialized countries in the proportion of national income given in aid to developing nations. Most foreign aid is given not for humanitarian reasons but to accomplish strategic and military objectives. To what degree would U.S. security interests be enhanced by a foreign policy constructed with major attention to development aid?

Evaluating international trade agreements according to their impact on the hungry. Exports are an important component of a nation's economy. Benefits from export products only assist the poor when they are shared broadly as part of a development program that brings jobs and income to those who would otherwise be hungry. Where it has been advantageous for U.S. companies to transfer production outside the U.S., it is necessary for government to enact measures that assist the local job market, provide job training, and ensure the domestic safety net. Trade agreements must be examined for their impact on labor, wages, environment, and children in all countries involved in the agreement. Fair trade agreements can make a significant influence on the well-being of the hungry.

Monitoring the effectiveness of state organized welfare programs. The 1996 welfare reform law relegated to states the authority for administering welfare, while reducing the amount of federal funding and setting new standards for the employment of welfare recipients. Equipping the poor to work requires a certain investment in job training, child care, health insurance, and transportation, provisions that are handled with different degrees of effectiveness in different states. Those concerned about the impact of welfare laws on the poor need to carefully monitor the impact of the new welfare programs, especially on the most vulnerable in society, mothers and children.

Promoting the development of more microenterprise credit. Small loans to low-income people can make an enormous difference in their attaining economic self-sufficiency. While large lending institutions typically refrain from lending to the poor, seeing them as bad credit risks, small loans to the poor make it possible for many to engage in productive business endeavors that allow a new level of financial independence. Repayment rates in microenterprise lending are comparatively high. An influx of capital in such lending would greatly enhance the capacity of the poor to fend for themselves.

Supporting sustainable agricultural practices. The "green revolution" has greatly expanded the capacity of farmers to feed the world's population. The scale of farming has, however, favored the development of corporate farming over the family farm. Not only in the U.S. but also in the developing world, the trend toward corporate farming is leading to the displacement of farm families from the land. In addition, the use of fertilizers and pesticides is leading to the degradation of the environment. It is important to hold in balance the value of efficiency in corporate farming with that of the integrity of farming on a smaller scale. What agricultural practices contribute most to the health of communities and the health of the environment?

Stewarding the usable water supply. Increasingly human communities are being threatened by water shortages. One-third of the world's harvest is grown on irrigated land. Seventy percent of the water drawn from rivers and underground sources is used for irrigation.[4] A greater concentration of people in urban areas puts extra pressure on the water supply in certain areas. Water tables are declining throughout the world and rivers are being consumed at alarming rates. Competition for water between urban and rural communities is a point of tension. Both water conservation measures and new technology for desalination of ocean water are urgently needed.

Expanding initiatives to improve health care and education. "Poor health care and little education hinder the ability of people to increase their earnings and provide adequately for their families."[15] Mental capacity is severely impaired by inadequate diet in childhood. There is an established correlation between poor health care and education as well as hunger and poverty. Wherever infant mortality, literacy, and school attendance rates improve, hunger and poverty rates decline. The greatest impact on the quality of life is made by the implementation of primary health care and primary education. Attention to the health and education of infants and small children contribute at a disproportionate rate to economic development. In many parts of the world (especially Africa), urgent attention needs to be given to the HIV/AIDS pandemic as a tremendous challenge to threatened economies.

Preferential concern for the well-being of children and women. The most innocent and vulnerable victims of the plague of malnutrition are the children. The United Nations introduced in the 1980s a fourfold approach to child survival that has proven extremely effective in combating the deadly combination of malnutrition and disease. The elements of this program are: 1) growth monitoring (tracking weight at regular intervals to ensure adequate nutrition), 2) oral rehydration therapy (providing a solution of salt and sugar in clean water to replenish children dehydrated by diarrhea), 3) breast feeding (greatly preferable to the cost and hygienic problems of baby formula) and 4) immunization (one vaccine can protect from seven common childhood diseases). In the U.S. the Special Supplemental Nutrition Program for Women, Infants, and Children (WIC) has been proven effective in reducing infant mortality and increasing school performance by children.

In addition to the special attention directed to the care of children, concern must be raised for the well-being of women. Women continue to suffer discrimination in wages, employment, education, land ownership, inheritance, and medical care. Each of these causes for discrimination leads to poverty and malnutrition among women at a disproportionate rate. Special educational and development projects directed at girls and women are indicated.

Following the direction of an established advocacy organization like Bread for the World will enhance advocacy efforts in these and related areas.[16] Members of Bread for the World are apprised regularly of current legislation and its implications for those who are hungry. Likewise the relief, educational, and advocacy efforts of denominational hunger programs are indispensable to the church's ministry on behalf of the hungry. For Lutherans, the ELCA World Hunger Program has an impeccable record for effectively addressing the needs of the hungry in a holistic way.[17] The ministry of the church in promoting relief and development efforts on behalf of the hungry must be coupled with strong advocacy that works toward a greater measure of social justice in the structures that order human society.

Spiritual courage

Already the churches have done much to assist in the effort to end world hunger. Church organizations are among the most effective in organizing development projects that take seriously the needs of the poorest and in providing hunger relief in times of famine. A church committed to ending hunger as a matter of *status confessionis* will multiply its resources for direct ministry in those places where hunger is most acute. It will work closely with people at the grassroots to ensure that its resources are employed to assist those most seriously affected by chronic malnutrition.

There will continue to be an urgent need for the church to be prepared and equipped to serve at short notice when famine threatens entire populations due to natural disasters (e.g., drought, flood) or social disasters (e.g., war, refugees). Food stockpiles must be made available quickly and negotiations with the relevant governments must be handled efficiently in order to deliver food relief to the hungry in a timely fashion when famine strikes. Many times church-related organizations are well-situated to intervene in a conflicted situation in order to supply food to the famished. Famine relief in times of disaster needs to remain an essential component of church-based hunger work. Yet only about 3% of the approximately seven million hunger-related deaths that occur in a typical year are the result of famines.[18] The vast majority of deaths to hunger are the result of poverty, chronic malnutrition, and the diseases that victimize the malnourished. This is the reason that the church must all the more focus its attention both on developmental projects that assist the hungry toward food self-sufficiency and on advocacy.

What would it take to see the virtual elimination of hunger in our world? According to Frances Moore Lappé, the primary missing ingredient is "moral courage":

> Our capacity to help end world hunger is infinite, for the roots of hunger touch every aspect of our lives—where we work, what we teach our children, how we fulfill our role as citizens, where we shop and save . . . So it takes courage to cry out, "The

emperor wears no clothes!" The world is awash in food, and all this suffering is the result of human decisions.[19]

In their extensive historical study of human hunger, the authors of *Hunger in History: Food Shortage, Poverty, and Deprivation* arrive at the conclusion that achieving an end to hunger is a realistic goal:

> Our perspective finds the demise of hunger attainable because for almost three decades now there may have been enough food in the world for all its people, the rudiments of an international safety net for the end of famine and food shortage is well in place, the proportion of households in food poverty is on the decline, and renewed international efforts to end food deprivation for children are under way. . .The demise of hunger may be attainable because for the first time in human history it is possible to contemplate the end of food scarcity, famine, and mass starvation . . . . The demise of hunger may be attainable because we know that the end of food poverty does not require the end of all poverty.[20]

We stand at an amazing juncture in human history. Just as certain diseases that once plagued humanity have been eliminated, so now we stand at the threshold of ending the plague of hunger.

What the church of Jesus Christ needs at this hour is not only moral courage but "spiritual courage." The Scriptures witness boldly to God's own concern for the poor and hungry. Jesus taught us, his disciples, the Lord's Prayer as a "justice prayer" that we pray regularly when we assemble. We are intimately connected with sister and brother Christians and other neighbors in the human family who testify to the acute needs of the hungry, those who are daily dying from our neglect. God has given us resources to be shared generously and wisely on behalf of the least of our brothers and sisters. God has placed us in a church where we have "companions" (literally, "those who break bread with us") on the journey. And God has given you a voice to cry out from the rooftops.

The Gospel of Jesus Christ comes to us as a free gift of grace that satisfies the hungers of the human heart. Jesus Christ feeds us with forgiveness, love, and the gift of eternal life, in order that we might be set free from preoccupation with our own neediness and turn and pay attention to the needs of our neighbors. Jesus Christ speaks to us who are in need of spiritual courage: "I have said this to you, so that in me you may have peace. In the world you face persecution. But take courage; I have conquered the world!" (John 16:33). We have everything we need. What is to prevent us giving them something to eat?

Questions for reflection and discussion

1. Why do most people think that ending hunger is not a real possibility? What do you think?
2. What does it mean to describe having sufficient food as a "human right"?
3. In a world with nearly one billion hungry people, what should Christians in the United States do to challenge the common understanding of food as a for-profit industry?
4. Why is it easier for Christians to engage in social service than in social advocacy? How does social advocacy fit into your understanding of Christian responsibility?
5. Which of the "ten key factors" for ending world hunger make the most sense to you? Which ones do you question?
6. What gives you spiritual courage? When do you need spiritual courage?

Conclusion

Kingdom of God and the Cross

To be confronted with the reality of massive hunger in our world and to hear God's word on behalf of justice for the poor leads us who are not hungry to be convicted by our sin. We see the effects of sin embedded in social, political, and economic structures. But we know finally that the roots of those sinful structures come out of the human heart—your heart and mine. To be moved by the plight of the suffering of the world is to be moved to confession of sin and repentance.

What is the connection between all that I have said in these pages and the cross of Jesus Christ? I make three concluding points.

First, the theology of the cross means God suffers with the poor. God's heart bleeds in the face of the suffering. When we go to respond to the hungry, God in Jesus Christ is already there to meet us.

Second, the theology of the cross, viewed from below in human terms, means we should understand why the Jesus who proclaimed the dawning of God's kingdom in his own words and actions ended up on a cross. To announce the arrival of God's reign is threatening to those in power. The sign written above the cross was intended to mock Jesus for presuming to proclaim that he brought the kingdom. It read, "The King of the Jews" (Mark 15:26).

Third, the theology of the cross, viewed from above in theological terms, means that God has chosen to save you and me and the entire world by the death and resurrection of this same Jesus Christ. On the cross, Jesus confronted and defeated all the principalities and powers that keep us in bondage to death and sin: our preoccupation with self, with security, with superiority (Col. 2:15). By raising Jesus from the dead, God sets us free from our bondage to sin in order to live in conformity with the way of Jesus. We die and rise each new morning in remembrance of our baptism.

Because you and I remain entangled in sin, *simul justus et peccator* ("simultaneously saint and sinner"), no amount of rallying around justice texts from the Bible is sufficient to set us free. While remembering our justice heritage is vital, something yet more radical is required. As I listen to myself making the case that justice for the poor and hungry belongs to the core of Scripture, I also have become aware of how accusing, harsh, and merciless those texts can sound. I stand convicted by my own words. Those who give leadership in the church already lead impossible lives. And to summon those same leaders to be responsible for feeding nearly one billion hungry neighbors appears to add one more impossible task.

There is finally only one solution to the impasse in which we find ourselves as we listen to God's word in its defense of the poor. There is finally only one way for camels to get through the eye of the needle. And so in conclusion, I want to declare to you, the reader, the most clear and radical word that I know that can free our church to serve the hungry:

> In the mercy of almighty God, Jesus Christ was given to die for you, and for his sake God forgives you all your sins. To those who believe in Jesus Christ, God gives the power to become the children of God and bestows on them the Holy Spirit.[1]

"For freedom Christ has set us free" (Gal. 5:1). Free to act.

Questions for reflection and discussion

1. What does Jesus dying on the cross have to do with the hungry people of our world?
2. How does hearing absolution set you free for serving your neighbor?

A Sermon Postscript
Through the Needle's Eye

Text: Matthew 19:23-26

Then Jesus said to his disciples, "Truly I tell you, it will be hard for a rich person to enter the kingdom of heaven. Again I tell you, it is easier for a camel to go through the eye of a needle than for someone who is rich to enter the kingdom of God." When the disciples heard this, they were greatly astounded and said, "Then who can be saved?" But Jesus looked at them and said, "For mortals it is impossible, but for God all things are possible."

Dear Sister and Brother Camels,

We are faced with a first order spiritual problem. When I use the word "spiritual," I refer to a problem that goes to the core of our existence: a problem that encompasses body, mind, heart, and soul—all that we are. We camels are voraciously hungry creatures: hungry for something to satisfy our deep aching need. We are hungry creatures: physically hungry but also hungry for eternal life, the kingdom of heaven.

In order to still our nagging hunger, we have taken up "the chase," the chase that entices us with the promise of fulfillment. Each camel has gone a separate way on the chase. Each one on the chase has become encumbered with a world of things. Look how your backs are weighed down with booty and dreams of booty. Look how you worry about your things: what you will eat, drink, and wear.

Here in this land we are very good at the chase; so good that our bellies are full. We hear troubling reports about other camels, those who have become victims of the chase. But what are they to us? We are on our own chase, they on theirs. We are satiated by our successes. Yawn! Let us be entertained! Let us develop a new age religion that can help us on the chase!

Brother and sister camels, I'm here today to tell you one of us has been to the other side. One of us has visited the other side and reports it's nothing like this land of the chase. The grass is long and luscious on the other side, and camels share the fields together. There is no hierarchy on the other side, only eagerness to perform humble tasks. There is no violence on the other side, no vengeance, no war. Camels admit their fallibility on the other side; a spirit of reconciliation prevails. On the other side, camels gather together to tell stories, listen to one another, and sing songs before they joyfully go about their days in loving concern for one another.

You ask the right question: "What is to prevent us from passing over to the other side?" Only one thing: to arrive there you have to get through the eye of this needle. "Impossible!" you say. For the eye of the needle is small. And we have become so very large. It's a first order spiritual problem: to let go of the baggage you have accumulated; to reduce your physical size to that of, say, a mustard seed; and, most difficult of all, to reduce the size of your ego, your attachment to the chase.

There is only one way to cast out the demon that possesses us, the demon of the chase that makes us so large. This one does not come out except by prayers and fasting (cf. Matt. 17:21).

Sister and brother camels, here are the words for the prayers, written in this holy book, the Bible. They speak of the one who has been to the other side. Other prayers are preserved in liturgy and song, prayers that invoke the name of the one who can make us small and escort us to the other side.

And here is the stuff for the feast, simple bread and wine, diet food for the kingdom, the only food that can make us thin enough for the eye of the needle.

Now is the time to be transformed—here and now—as often as we gather together to share the prayers and eat this meal. Hear this poem by Stephen Mitchell:

Lying back on the unbelievably lush grass,
he remembers: all those years
(how excruciating they were!)
of fasting and one-pointed concentration,
until finally he was thin enough:
thaumaturgically thin,
thread thin, almost unrecognizable in his camelness:
until the moment in front of the unblinking eye,
when he put his front hooves together.
Took one long last breath.
Aimed. Dived.
The exception may prove the rule, but what proves the exception?

"It is not that such things are possible," the camel thinks, smiling.
"But such things are possible for me." [1]

"Through the Eye of the Needle" by Stephen Mitchell, © 1991
THEOLOGY TODAY 48 (1991): 73.
Reprinted with permission.

Addendum:
On *Status Confessionis*

In 1997 the Evangelical Lutheran Church in America responded to memorials from synods that urged the adoption of ending hunger as a matter of *status confessionis*. The term, *status confessionis*, comes from the Formula of Concord but took on new significance in the twentieth century.

As I understand it, there are two types of interpretation:

1. A time for confessing church exists when the church's freedom to preach the gospel is threatened by the state. Such a situation appeared in Nazi Germany when the German Christians attempted to coerce the church and make it an arm of the state. For example, Karl Barth and Dietrich Bonhoeffer took this position in Nazi Germany with regard to the takeover of the church by the German Christians.

2. A time for confessing church exists when the church stands under an imperative to oppose a great moral evil. Dietrich Bonhoeffer's opposition to the Nazi regime because of its persecution of the Jews, extended his opposition to the Third Reich not only because of its co-opting of the church but also because of the moral evil being perpetrated. This type of position was adopted by the Lutheran World Federation meeting at Dar es Salaam in 1977. The resolution passed there was not just about the oppression of the church but a summons to the church to oppose the evil of apartheid:

> Under normal circumstances Christians may have different opinions in political questions. However, political and social systems may become so perverted and oppressive that it is consistent with the confession to reject them and to work for

changes. We especially appeal to our white member Churches in South Africa to recognize that the situation in Southern Africa constitutes a status confessionis. This means that, on the basis of faith and in order to manifest the unity of the Church, Churches would publicly and unequivocally reject the existing apartheid system.[1]

Here *status confessionis* is dealt with as a larger ethical question.

The Memorials Committee opposed the adoption of the *status confessionis* measure, giving as its rationale that trying to attain consensus on *status confessionis* could be a distraction from the real task of responding to the hungry. If this were indeed the case, I would be the first to say this is a path we should not begin to go down. The Memorials Committee was correct that such a proposal transcends the purview of the ELCA and would require discussion in the global Lutheran communion and ecumenically. But it was incorrect in its interpretation of the South African resolution: the issue was not just about the oppression of the church under apartheid; it was about opposition to apartheid in principle. In this way the Lutheran World Federation resolution could be restated:

We especially appeal to our wealthy member churches in the First World to recognize that the situation of massive world hunger constitutes a status confessionis. This means that, on the basis of faith and in order to manifest the unity of the Church, Churches would publicly and unequivocally reject the existing economic status quo.

Clearly, the implementation of a resolution to declare opposition to hunger as a matter of *status confessionis* would require the mobilization of the Evangelical Lutheran Church in America to partnership internationally with the churches of the Lutheran

World Federation and domestically with its ecumenical partners. It would require that we as a church in the United States first resolve to see hunger eliminated in our own country, starting with the counties and states where our congregations are located.

The goal of ending world hunger is not a utopian dream. Groups such as Bread for the World (with its 2003 Offering of Letters) have set ending hunger as a program goal. The time has come for the church, based on its biblical and theological tradition, to employ its resources in a concerted effort to eliminate the moral evil of hunger. What resources, if not *status confessionis*, do we have in the Lutheran theological tradition to address this scandal?

Bibliography

Beckmann, David and Arthur Simon. 1999. *Grace at the Table: Ending Hunger in God's World.* New York: Paulist Press.

Boucher, Douglas H. (editor). 1999. *The Paradox of Plenty: Hunger in a Bountiful World.* Oakland, CA: FoodFirst Books.

Brown, Robert McAfee. (editor). 1990. *Kairos: Three Prophetic Challenges to the Church.* Grand Rapids, MI: Eerdmans.

Critser, Greg. 2003. *Fat Land: How Americans Became the Fattest People in the World.* Boston: Houghton Mifflin Company.

Duchrow, Ulrich. (David Lewis, translator). 1987. *Global Economy: A Confessional Issue for the Churches?* Geneva: WCC Publications.

Guhrt, Joachim. "*Status Confessionis:* The Witness of a Confessing Church," in *Reformed World* 37 (Dec 83): 301-308.

Hunsinger, George. "Barth, Barmen and the Confessing Church Today," in *Katallagete 9* (Summer 85):14-27. The entire issue of *Katallagete 10* (Fall 87) is devoted to responses to Hunsinger's article.

Lappé, Frances Moore and Joseph Collins. 1978. *Food First: Beyond the Myth of Scarcity.* New York: Ballantine.

Lappé, Frances Moore, Joseph Collins, and Peter Rosset. 1998. *World Hunger: Twelve Myths.* New York: Grove Press.

Lorenz, Eckehart. (editor). 1983. *The Debate on Status Confessionis: Studies in Christian Political Theology.* Geneva: Lutheran World Federation.

Lutz, Charles P. 1994. *Loving Neighbors Far and Near: U.S. Lutherans Respond to a Hungry World.* Minneapolis: Augsburg Fortress.

Moe-Lobeda, Cynthia D. 2002. *Healing a Broken World: Globalization and God.* Minneapolis: Fortress Press.

Newman, Lucile F. (General Editor). 1990. *Hunger in History: Food Shortage, Poverty, and Deprivation.* Cambridge: Basil Blackwell.

Sider, Ronald J. (editor). 1980. *Cry Justice: The Bible on Hunger and Poverty.* Downers Grove, IL: InterVarsity Press.

Sider, Ronald J. 1990. *Rich Christians in an Age of Hunger.* Dallas: Word Publishing.

Simon, Arthur. 2003. *How Much Is Enough? Hungering for God in an Affluent Culture.* Grand Rapids, MI: Baker Books.

Visser't Hooft, W. A. 1973. *Memoirs.* Philadelphia: Westminster Press.

Notes

Introduction

1   Enrique Dussel, *A History of the Church in Latin America: Colonialism to Liberation (1492-1979)*, trans. Alan Neely (Grand Rapids: Eerdmans, 1981), p. 307.

Chapter 1

1   Martin Luther, "The Freedom of a Christian," in Timothy F. Lull, ed., *Martin Luther's Basic Theological Writings* (Minneapolis: Fortress, 1989), p. 596.

2   Ernst Käsemann, *Jesus Means Freedom*, trans. Frank Clarke (Philadelphia: Fortress, 1972).

3   Dietrich Bonhoeffer, *The Cost of Discipleship*, trans. R. H. Fuller (New York: Macmillan, 1963), pp. 45ff.

4   Bruce Chilton, *Pure Kingdom* (Grand Rapids: Eerdmans, 1996), pp. 23-44.

5   Norman Perrin, *Jesus and the Language of the Kingdom: Symbol and Metaphor in New Testament Interpretation* (Philadelphia: Fortress, 1976).

Chapter 2

1   Quoted in Robert Gibbs, *Correlations in Rosenzweig and Levinas* (Princeton: Princeton University Press, 1992), p. 257, making reference to this quote in Levinas.

2   Martin Luther, "*The Large Catechism*", in Robert Kolb and Timothy J. Wengert, eds., *The Book of Concord: The Confessions of the Evangelical Lutheran Church* (Minneapolis: Fortress, 2000), p. 445 (43).

3 The radicality of a prayer for the forgiveness of "debts" was so shocking that even Matthew (6:14-15) needed to offer interpretation.

4 Sharon H. Ringe, *Jesus, Liberation, and the Biblical Jubilee: Images for Ethics and Christology*, (Philadelphia: Fortress, 1985), pp. 81-84.

5 Martin Luther, "The Large Catechism," in *The Book of Concord*, p. 452 (84).

6 Richard A. Hoehn, "Introduction" in Bread for the World, *The Changing Politics of Hunger: Ninth Annual Report on the State of World Hunger* (Silver Spring, MD: Bread for the World Institute, 1998), p. 2.

7   Martin Luther, "The Small Catechism," in *The Book of Concord*, p. 357 (14).

Chapter 3

1   Quoted in Emmanuel Levinas, *Totality and Infinity* (Pittsburgh: Duquenes University Press, 1969), p. 201.

2   Dietrich Bonhoeffer, *Letters and Papers from Prison*, ed. Eberhard Bethge (New York: Macmillan, 1972), p. 17.

3   Phil Hefner, "The Church as a Community of Belonging in a Society Divided by Economic and Social Class," *Currents in Theology and Mission* 24 (June 97):220.

4   *Sufficient, Sustainable Livelihood for All*, A Social Statement on Economic Life, adopted by the Evangelical Lutheran Church in America at Churchwide Assembly on August 20, 1999.

5   Martin Luther King, Jr., *A Testament of Hope: The Essential Writings of Martin Luther King, Jr.*, ed. James Melvin Washington (San Francisco: Harper & Row, 1986), p. 501.

Chapter 4

1   An abbreviated version of this chapter first appeared as an article in *Lutheran Partners 13*, No. 3 (May/June 97):33-37.

2   These statistics are taken from Bread for the World, "Hunger Basics," http://www.bread.org/hungerbasics.

3   Ron Sider, *Cry Justice: The Bible on Hunger and Poverty* (Downers Grove, IL: InterVarsity Press, 1980).

4   *Catechism of the Catholic Church* (Mahwah, NJ: Paulist Press, 1994), p. 589.

5   Robert Kolb and Timothy J. Wengert, eds., *The Book of Concord: The Confessions of the Evangelical Lutheran Church* (Minneapolis: Fortress Press, 2000), p. 637 (10).

6   W.A. Visser't Hooft, *Memoirs* (Philadelphia: Westminster Press, 1973), p. 363.

7   John W. DeGruchy and Charles Villa-Vicencio, eds., *Apartheid is a Heresy* (Grand Rapids: Eerdmans, 1983), pp. 160f.

8   Eckehart Lorenz, "The Criteria of Status Confessionis." *Lutheran Forum* 17 (Advent 83): 20-22.

9   Robert McAfee Brown, ed., *Kairos: Three Prophetic Challenges to the Church* (Grand Rapids: Eerdmans, 1990).

10 George Hunsinger, "Barth, Barmen and the Confessing Church Today," *Katallagete* 9, No. 2 (Summer 85):14-27.

11 Ulrich Duchrow, *Global Economy: A Confessional Issue for the Churches?*, trans. David Lewis (Geneva: WCC Publications, 1987).

Chapter 5

1 Frances Moore Lappé, Joseph Collins, and Peter Rosset, *World Hunger: Twelve Myths* (New York: Grove Press, 1998), p. 8.

2 Ibid., pp.106-107.

3 Bread for the World, *The Changing Politics of Hunger: Ninth Annual Report on the State of World Hunger* (Silver Springs, MD: Bread for the World Institute, 1998), pp. 10 and 13.

4 Ibid., p. 13.

5 For this and the following cf. David Beckmann and Art Simon, *Grace at the Table: Ending Hunger in God's World* (New York: Paulist Press, 1999), pp. 174-176.

6 Ibid., p. 176.

7 Cf. Shannon Jung, *Food for Life: Eating and the Goodness of God* (Minneapolis: Fortress Press, 2004).

8 On the church's role in social advocacy cf. Craig L. Nessan, *Beyond Maintenance to Mission: A Theology of the Congregation* (Minneapolis: Fortress Press, 1999), pp. 113-119.

9 "Engaging Economic Globalization as a Communion: A Working Paper of the Lutheran World Federation" (Geneva: The Lutheran World Federation, 2001), p. 21.

10 Ibid., p. 22.

11 For the following, see the analysis by Beckmann and Simon, *Grace at the Table.*

12 For a rich discussion of globalization, see Cynthia D. Moe-Lobeda, *Healing a Broken World: Globalization and God* (Minneapolis: Fortress Press, 2002).

13 Beckmann and Simon, *Grace at the Table*, p. 116.

14 Ibid., p. 68.

15 Ibid., p. 81.

16 Contact Bread for the World at www.bread.org or call 1-800-82-BREAD or write to 50 F Street NW, Suite 500, Washington, DC 20001.

17 Contact the ELCA World Hunger Appeal at www.elca.org/hunger or write to 8765 West Higgins Road, Chicago, Illinois 60631.

18 Beckmann and Simon, *Grace at the Table*, p. 19.

19 Lappé, Collins, and Rosset, *World Hunger*, p. 178.

20 Lucille F. Newman, general ed., *Hunger in History: Food Shortage, Poverty, and Deprivation* (Cambridge: Basil Blackwell, 1990), p. 404.

Conclusion

1 *Lutheran Book of Worship* (Minneapolis: Augsburg, 1978), p. 56.

A Sermon Postscript

1 Stephen Mitchell, "Through the Eye of the Needle," *Theology Today* 48 (April 1991): 73.

Addendum: On *Status Confessionis*

1 John W. DeGruchy and Charles Villa-Vicencio, eds., *Apartheid Is a Heresy* (Grand Rapids: Eerdmans, 1983), pp. 160f.

OTHER LUTHERAN VOICES TITLES

Large-quantity purchases or custom editions of these books are available at a discount from the publisher. For more information, contact the sales department at Augsburg Fortress, Publishers, 1-800-328-4648, or write to: Sales Director, Augsburg Fortress, Publishers, P.O. Box 1209, Minneapolis, MN 55440-1209.

See www.lutheranvoices.com